QUILT IT!

Appliqué quilt made by Ann King, Northampton

QUILT IT!

*Quilting ideas and inspiration
for patchwork and appliqué*

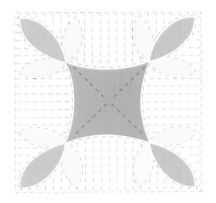

BARBARA CHAINEY

BOTHELL, WASHINGTON

A DAVID & CHARLES BOOK

First published in the UK in 1999

ISBN 1-56477-276-4

Photography by Mark Wood
Book design by Glynis Edwards

Printed in Singapore by Imago
for David & Charles
Brunel House   Newton Abbot   Devon

03 02 01 00 9 8 7 6 5 4

Martingale & Company
PO Box 118
Bothell, WA 98041-0118
www.patchwork.com

MISSION STATEMENT

WE ARE DEDICATED TO PROVIDING QUALITY PRODUCTS
AND SERVICE BY WORKING TOGETHER TO INSPIRE
CREATIVITY AND TO ENRICH THE LIVES WE TOUCH.

CONTENTS

INTRODUCTION   7

SOME BASICS   8

SINGLE BLOCKS   12
Pieced blocks   14
Curved-seam blocks   22
Appliqué blocks   26
Strip-pieced blocks   30
Foundation-pieced blocks   31

COMBINING BLOCKS   32
Four blocks   32
Full quilt, blocks set edge to edge   42
Full quilt using two blocks   64
Main block and plain block   72
Blocks set on point   90
Square medallion setting   104
Sampler quilts   118
Log cabin quilts   124
Strip-pieced quilts   128

ONE-SHAPE QUILTS   137

AMISH-STYLE QUILTS   142

SASHINGS AND BORDERS   146

PATTERNS   176

MARKING METHODS AND MARKERS   185

HAND AND MACHINE QUILTING   188

SELECTED BIBLIOGRAPHY AND   190
ACKNOWLEDGEMENTS

INDEX   191

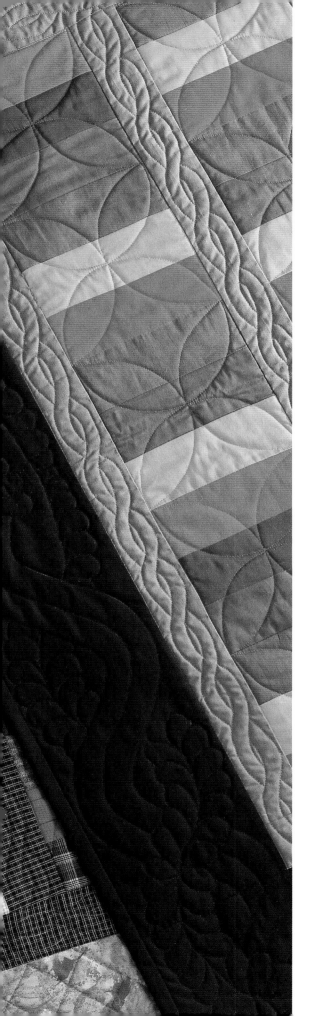

INTRODUCTION

Much time, thought and effort goes into the planning and making of a quilt – and maybe even some blood, sweat and tears. And most of us experience that all too familiar lurch of uncertainty when we survey the top and wonder what to quilt and where – is there a secret formula only revealed to a chosen few (those who win ribbons at shows)? What are the options other than outline quilting? What sort of patterns will work best? Where should the patterns go? Will it look "right"? We recognise that quilting should complement and enhance the work already done whether it is piecing, appliqué or a mixture of both, but where do we go from there?

This book was begun as an answer to the "how do I quilt it?" questions I had heard being asked in classes and quilting groups during the course of the past sixteen years. It has proved to be a steep but rewarding learning curve as to what computer graphics and quilting programs can achieve and it became apparent quite early on that it would be impossible to make the finished book truly comprehensive without it being too heavy to lift. So, I have limited the scope of what follows to main pointers and ideas that are easy to draft and stitch, using a minimum of math, geometry and complicated tools, and which are suitable for hand and machine quilters of all skill levels. The emphasis throughout is on self-help rather than using purchased patterns, and all of the ideas presented here are straightforward to quilt by hand or machine and can be used as shown or taken as a starting point to create your own unique quilting patterns.

A short review of some of the basic principles and considerations for planning quilting precedes the first main section, which looks at a selection of blocks and explores some of the possibilities for quilting. Branching out to put four blocks together and quilt them is covered in section two, progressing to a wide variety of full-size quilts in the third and main section. Devising quilting for sashings and borders is discussed in section four, while practicalities of marking, markers, and hand and machine quilting are the subject of section five. Finally, a selection of easy-to-draft quilting patterns has been included for you to use or adapt to suit your needs. You can dip in and out of each section, or just start at the beginning and go on to the end – either way, I hope you will discover just how easy it is to make your own quilting plans.

Simple strip quilts, fabric selection by Mandy Fanthom, machine quilted by Sally Radway

SOME BASICS

IN GENERAL

One of the unsung benefits of quilting is that it can often gloss over a multitude of small imperfections in the block or quilt construction – seams that almost meet precisely, points that are only slightly blunt. Hand quilting allows you time to coax, push and pull any such "difficult" areas as you are stitching. Machine quilting is a much faster stitching process, but whichever quilting technique you use, blocks or quilts that are less than perfectly straight and have unexpected billows and ripples can often be straightened and de-rippled by carefully placed and spaced quilting, hence the expression "It'll quilt out".

If you need to straighten out a less than perfectly smooth quilt top, you may find that a medium to high density spread of texture will achieve the desired effect – more lines of quilting mean more shrinkage and control. Take care when planning the direction in which the lines will be stitched and try to work towards the free outer edges wherever possible, remembering that changes in quilting direction can result in small ripples between the lines. Whether you quilt by hand or machine, the fabric is pushed slightly ahead of the needle in the direction of the line you are stitching. If your lines are all worked in the same direction, the finished effect will be ripple free; if you have worked in alternating and opposing directions, this may not be the case.

BALANCE

In the past decade machine quilting has become more and more popular and quite rightly so. Now we have the chance to finish at least half the quilts we want to make in our lifetime rather than accumulating heaps of ideas and unquilted tops. There have also been wonderful advances in mechanical technology – sewing machines are better than ever and some virtually do everything including walking the dog. The net result is that more of us are quilting with improved machines and more of us are putting more quilted texture into our work.

Vermicelli or meander quilting is so easy to do on a sewing machine with the feed dogs dropped or covered that it is a favourite texture choice for all machine quilters irrespective of their level of experience. Meandering is a great way to practise free-motion machine quilting, and it usually looks highly effective, but you need to exercise a little caution with regard to the density or closeness of the continuously moving line – it is all too easy to overwork this texture and have it out of balance with the other quilted areas.

As with single blocks, a successfully quilted quilt has an appearance of evenness and balance of texture across the whole piece, without any part looking unfinished or "billowy". It is preferable to have very simple quilting spread evenly across the surface than a number of intensely quilted areas separated by large unquilted areas.

CUES AND CLUES

Consider the style of the quilt blocks themselves – are they traditional, contemporary or abstract in appearance? Are the blocks complex, with many pieces or a variety of shapes? Could one of the shapes be adapted and arranged into a complementary quilting pattern? Is there any one element or area that seems to be a natural focus that could be emphasised? If the block patterns are representational rather than abstract – sailing boats, cats or flowers for instance – then you already have some strong cues and clues to work with and develop as a theme.

Traditional-style quilts often call for traditional-style quilting. If old or reproduction fabrics have been used, you will perhaps want to consider quilting patterns that further emphasise this effect. You may also be more inclined to favour hand quilting rather than machine quilting as your stitching technique. On the other hand, a traditional-style quilt made with very contemporary fabric may give you scope to choose between hand and machine quilting and to take a less traditional approach to the quilting designs.

Apart from the style of the quilt, the fabrics used can help guide you in deciding where and what to quilt. For instance, if there is a predominance of fabrics with metallic accents and little plain or contrasting fabric, then it might be appropriate to use an overall quilting design in metallic thread. Look to see if there is a motif on any of the fabrics that might lend itself to being adapted for a quilting pattern – a flower, a leaf or perhaps a star or a swirl.

As an example of picking up cues and clues from the style of the quilt top, let's look at the three quilts on page 6. They are identical in construction – rectangles joined into three long strips, divided by sashing strips and finished with a deep border. The "feel" of each quilt is, however, quite different – pastel and floral, plaid and country, plain and strong colour. How would you have gone about planning the quilting? The pastel/floral quilt includes a number of fabrics that have a medium to large-scale pattern and the overall effect is less defined than either the country or the bright quilt. Complex and intricate quilting would not have shown to best advantage in this instance, so what I call the halving principle (see page 10) was used to create a large-scale grid on each of the three main strips and also to make simple sashing and border designs. The use of plaids and checks in the second quilt give it a country charm, but you can be sure that complex quilting will not show well – simple texture is more in keeping with the quilt's rustic character. A medium-scale clamshell pattern was chosen for the three main strips, with the curving lines making a good contrast with the straight lines of the piecing and echoing the curved lines of the small cable in the sashings and inner border. Notice how invisible the cable pattern is in comparison to the plain quilt where exactly the same pattern has been used in the same position. The third quilt has a contemporary Amish feel to it and the quilting has been designed to reflect this – a large-scale wineglass pattern in each of the three main strips, a small cable in the sashings and inner border, and a feathered cable pattern filling the deep outer border – all patterns that are associated with the Amish tradition. The

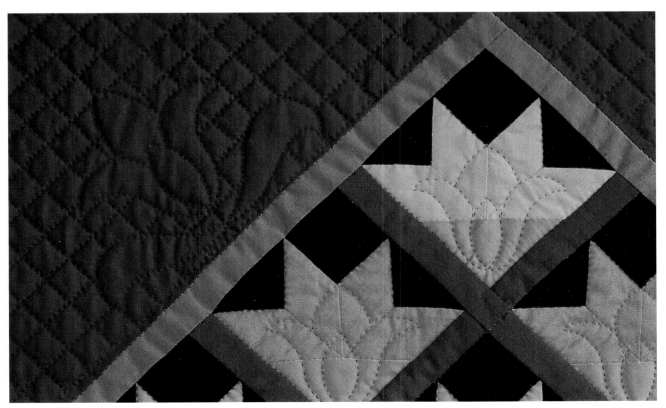

Cues and clues from the colours and style of piecing – plain vibrant colours and stylised lily pieced blocks give a contemporary Amish feel to this quilt made by Sandie Lush. The curving lines of the lily quilting motif contrast with the straight edges of the piecing as well as adding character and textural interest.

use of plain fabrics means that all the machine quilted texture shows clearly and crisply.

One of the main reasons why we ask the question "How do I quilt it?" is that visualising how quilting patterns and ideas will look on a block or quilt is not always easy. You may find that working with a rough sketch (or a photocopy or computer print-out) of the block or quilt is a good way to try out and develop some ideas. For a single block or small area of a quilt, you could also make an over-lay of tracing paper and map out some lines on it to give you an idea of how they would work.

If you think you would like to use a particular motif, try cutting a number of rough outlines of it from scrap paper so that you can place the shapes on the quilt and experiment with arranging them in different ways. This is also a good way of checking that the scale of the motif is appropriate for the overall piece. Using cut paper shapes in this way can also help you decide which motif

The plain spaces in this small quilt were filled with a simple spider-web pattern using the halving principle as a line placement guide. Notice how the border quilting picks up and reflects the same type of curve. Machine quilting by Sally Radway.

looks better if you are trying to find the best option from an initial selection of three or four. A particular and special merit of playing with scissors and scrap paper is that you can easily create some basic shapes (remember cutting snowflakes at school?) which can then be developed into your own quilting patterns by adding a few simple lines.

A good alternative to playing with cut paper shapes is to use a chalk wheel or pencil to draft rough out-lines and patterns directly onto the fabric (see section on Marking and Markers). You do not have to make precise or accurate marks when you do this, but it will give you an instant visual check on how certain patterns and styles of texture will look on a particular piece, and of course the lines can easily be erased and redrafted to try out other ideas.

Throughout the following pages you will find numerous references to something I call the halv-ing principle – here's an idea of how it works:

- Divide a square vertically once using a straight line
- Divide the same square horizontally once using a straight line
- Divide the square diagonally once, then twice using straight lines
- Divide square vertically using curved line
- Divide square horizontally using curved line
- Divide square diagonally once, then twice using curved lines
- Divide square vertically and horizontally using straight lines, then divide diagonally using curved lines.

All the main shapes of a block or blocks will bene-fit from being defined by outline or skeleton quilt-ing before doing anything further. Whether you decide to quilt exactly on the seam or slightly to one side is really a matter of personal preference or convenience, and the position of the seam allowances will mean that you will not necessarily achieve your highest quilting quality. Outline quilting does not always appear to add a great deal, but it does give vital and subtle definition as a basis on which to build as well as "controlling" the seams so that they lie as flat as possible. Once the outlining is done, you can turn your attentions to adding the icing on the cake.

The halving principle used again as a line placement guide for the curved windmill quilting pattern in each of the strip-pieced blocks. Echoing straight lines fill the black triangles and the border is worked in a cable variation. Machine quilting by Sally Radway.

The simplest quilting solutions are often the best. Curved lines will give a good contrast with the straight edges and sharp points of piecing. Straight lines will add texture and can make the most basic pieced design look more complex than it actually is.

In many cases, postponing decisions can work very well. If you can look at a single block or full-size quilt top and know immediately what to quilt where, then you are one in a million and should not be reading this. Adopting a "wait and see" attitude is not always a comfortable thing to do – most of us feel that we should have all our quilting decisions made before going on to put the three layers together and begin the actual stitching. But if you can persuade yourself to put the layers together and do the outline quilting first, and then be prepared to mark a little, stitch a little and mark a little more you may arrive by easy stages at a very pleasing quilting solution – this is "quilt as you go" in a very different guise, probably better described as "decide as you go". This approach also means that you don't spend hours agonising before you actually get to the quilting and there may be some happy surprises along the way. Having everything planned out down to the last and smallest line before you begin means that there is only the process of quilting to enjoy – with "decide as you go" you have a more flexible approach that allows you to make changes and improvements as the project progresses.

Above all, remember that there is no one correct answer to "How do I quilt it?". Instead there are any number of possibilities, some of which may appeal more than others. If you achieve an even balance of texture with a quilting treatment that pleases you, that is all there is to it.

SINGLE BLOCKS

What is a block? A block is a unit of patchwork or appliqué, often square, which can be used on its own or repeated a number of times to join together to make a quilt top.

What is the point of quilting single blocks? In the same way that you can try out different techniques for piecing and appliqué by making single blocks, quilting on this small scale is a great way to develop your hand and machine quilting skills. Single blocks that are larger than six inches square are a very manageable size to hand or machine quilt, although you may find that hand quilting and miniature-scale blocks (three inches square or less) are not always comfortable companions. Whilst it is not a rule (after all, in quilting there are no rules) it is an accepted generality that for miniature work the crisp sharp lines of machine quilting are often a better solution than the softer lines of hand quilting. Quilting individual or single blocks means that you can experiment with placement and style of quilting lines, marking methods and markers, needles, threads, battings and all the other choices involved in quilting, so that by the time you are ready to quilt a full-sized piece, you have established your skills and preferences. And it is always fascinating to see how even the plainest block can be enhanced and often transformed by some judiciously placed quilting before being finished as a cushion, pillow or bag.

Most quilters could produce a variety of unquilted single blocks from a "collection" built up over the years! Contributors to this arrangement include Sandie Lush, Patricia Cox, Linda Gabrielse.

PIECED BLOCKS

Pieced blocks obviously have seams and these create the skeleton or framework of the block, which you can treat as your basic design grid. You can either work with this skeleton or ignore it completely when planning how you will quilt a particular block.

Outline quilting is a good place to start – in fact, it is probably the best place to start every time. While it doesn't seem to add anything new to the block, it gives it a basic definition on which you can build and, without it, the finished result can seem to lack that certain something. Outline quilting requires little or no marking, and also while you are doing it, you can be thinking about what other quilting you will do.

There may be more than one interesting shape or area in a block, particularly if it has a complex structure. Look at the block from both close and long range to help you

Identify which shape(s) you want to emphasise – this may help you decide how much quilting to add, what it should be and where it should go.

Closely spaced or dense quilting over an area will make it appear to recede, allowing the area or shape immediately adjacent to it to come forward and be emphasised. If you decide to use close quilting in some areas, try not to leave any of the main shapes completely empty. Otherwise the overall balance of quilting will be uneven.

A subtle way of confirming or emphasising a particular shape is to add a second line of quilting just inside the outline quilting – the two lines can be up to a quarter of an inch apart if you wish.

The simplest of curved lines can give a strong feeling of movement and additional interest to almost any block – it may be something to do with the contrast between the predominantly straight edges of the piecing and the curve itself, but there is no doubt that the addition of just a few curves can dramatically alter the perception of a block pattern.

The bigger, fewer or simpler the shapes in a particular block, the more scope you have for quilting and the more you can change the overall look of that block with the texture you add.

FIG 1

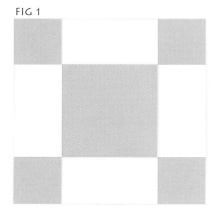
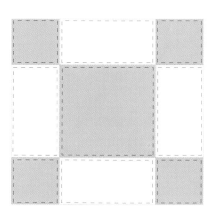

◀ FIG 1 This nine-patch block is very simple but can easily be made to look more complex by the addition of straight lines, curved lines, or a combination of both. Notice how the curved lines give a strong feeling of movement to the block.

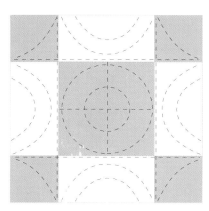
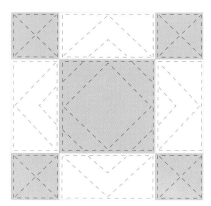
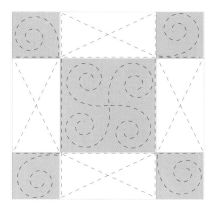

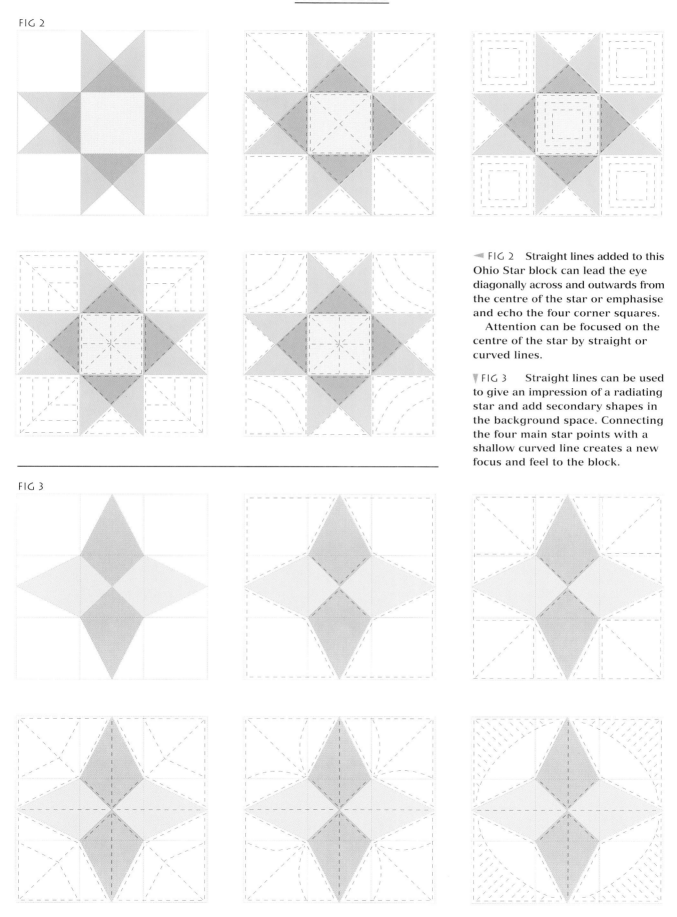

FIG 2

FIG 3

◀ FIG 2   Straight lines added to this Ohio Star block can lead the eye diagonally across and outwards from the centre of the star or emphasise and echo the four corner squares.

Attention can be focused on the centre of the star by straight or curved lines.

▼ FIG 3   Straight lines can be used to give an impression of a radiating star and add secondary shapes in the background space. Connecting the four main star points with a shallow curved line creates a new focus and feel to the block.

FIG 4

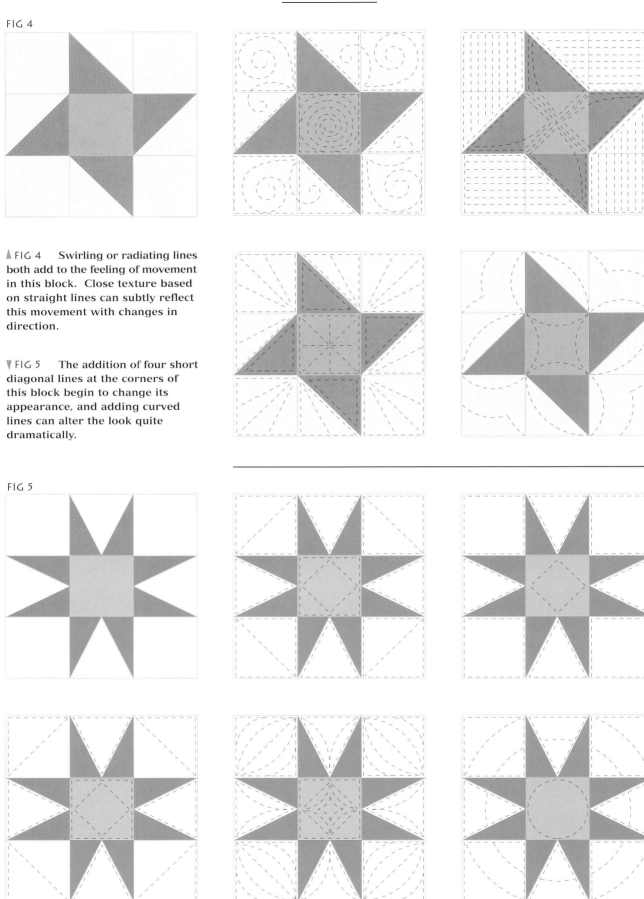

▲ FIG 4 Swirling or radiating lines both add to the feeling of movement in this block. Close texture based on straight lines can subtly reflect this movement with changes in direction.

▼ FIG 5 The addition of four short diagonal lines at the corners of this block begin to change its appearance, and adding curved lines can alter the look quite dramatically.

FIG 5

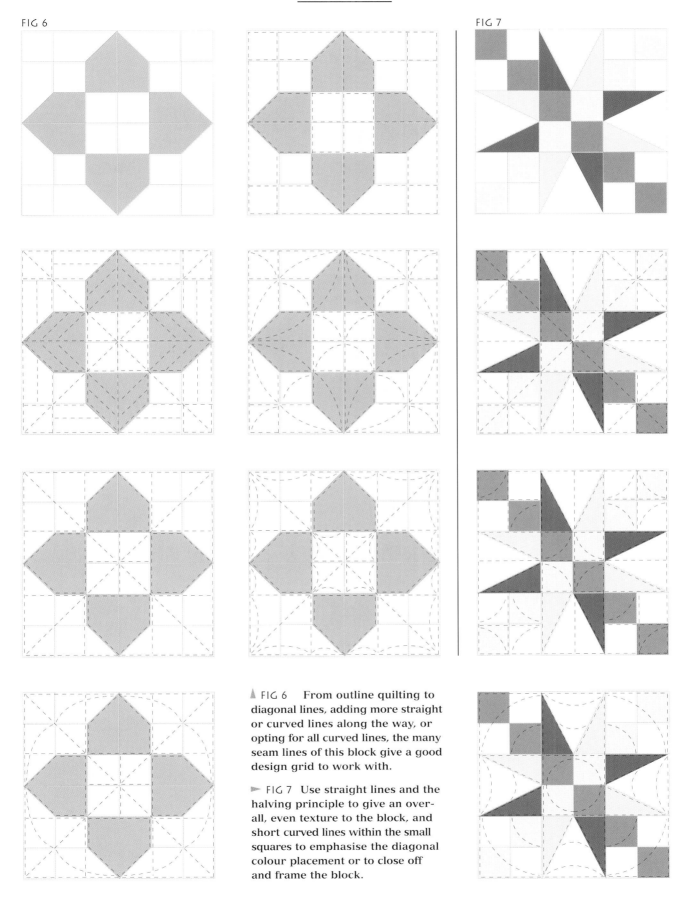

FIG 6

FIG 7

▲ FIG 6   From outline quilting to diagonal lines, adding more straight or curved lines along the way, or opting for all curved lines, the many seam lines of this block give a good design grid to work with.

➤ FIG 7   Use straight lines and the halving principle to give an over-all, even texture to the block, and short curved lines within the small squares to emphasise the diagonal colour placement or to close off and frame the block.

FIG 8

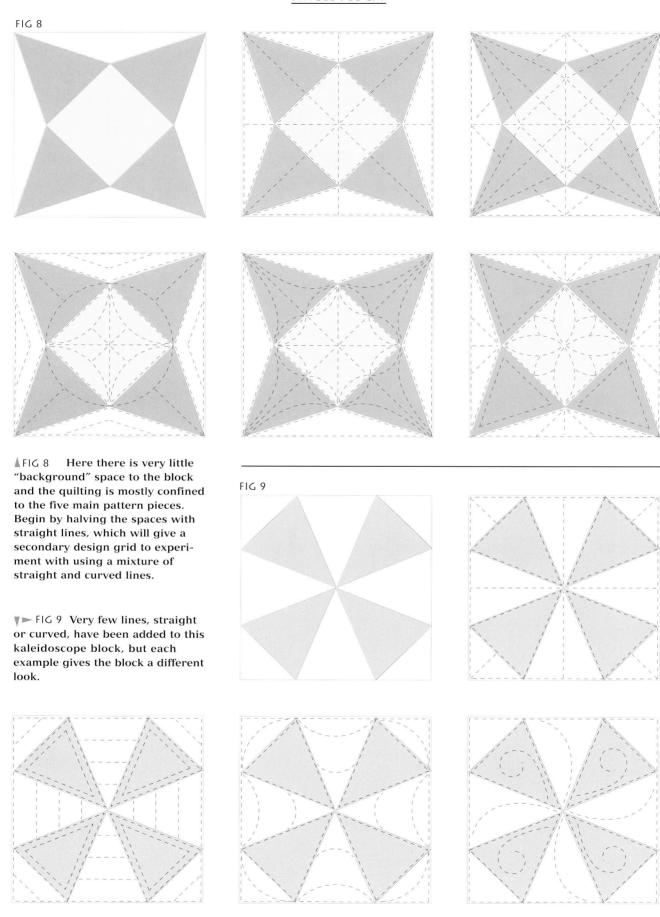

▲ FIG 8   Here there is very little "background" space to the block and the quilting is mostly confined to the five main pattern pieces. Begin by halving the spaces with straight lines, which will give a secondary design grid to experiment with using a mixture of straight and curved lines.

▼ ► FIG 9   Very few lines, straight or curved, have been added to this kaleidoscope block, but each example gives the block a different look.

FIG 9

FIG 10

FIG 11

▲ FIG 11 Simple shapes simply divided can look effective, irrespective of whether straight or curved lines are used.

◀ FIG 10 From basic outline quilting it is no great leap to a more complex appearance, which can be achieved by using the halving principle and short curved lines.

FIG 12

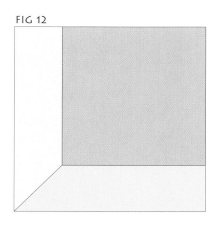 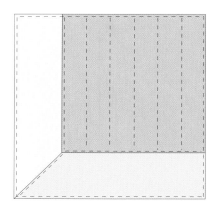 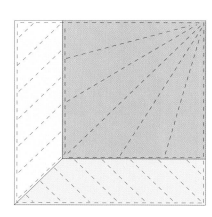

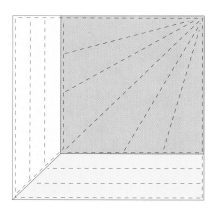 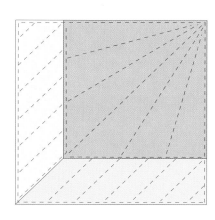

◀▼FIG 12 Blocks that have a strong 3-D element to them, such as this Attic Window block, often require only simple quilting, which could be based on straight lines as in this figure or on curves. The main square or "window" would be a good location for a motif or a design of your own based on the halving principle.

FIG 13

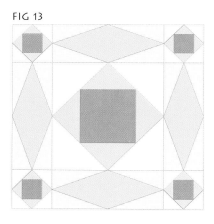 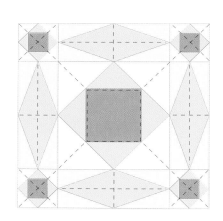

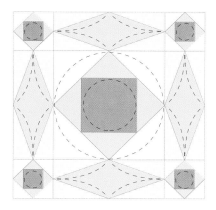 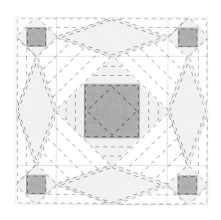

◀ FIG 13 A single Storm at Sea block has many seam allowances to consider but careful placement of either straight or curved lines within the shapes will make quilting easier. Both the basic diagonal and curved line suggestions shown here add a sense of direction and movement to the block, as does the use of parallel lines – remember that more quilting lines mean that particular area will appear to recede.

FIG 14

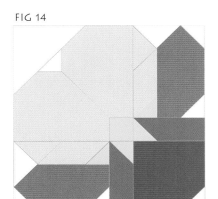
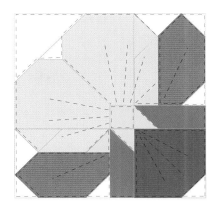

FIG 15

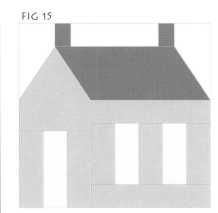

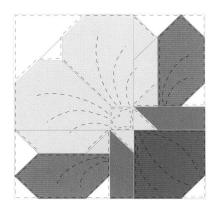

▲ FIG 14 Strongly graphic and representational blocks such as this 1930s Pansy designed by Ruby McKim may require only minimal quilting to enhance and emphasise their character – here the choice would be between straight or curved lines to break up the main areas.

► FIG 15 The traditional School-house block, like the McKim pansy, probably only requires a little quilting in addition to outlining – by suggesting roof texture etc. – to develop its character and style.

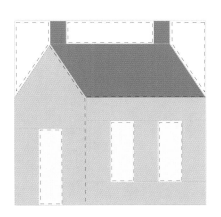

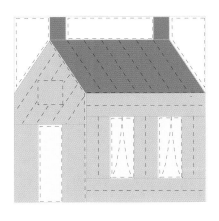

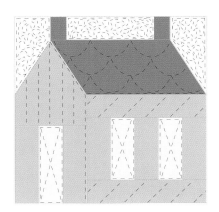

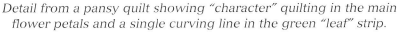

Detail from a pansy quilt showing "character" quilting in the main flower petals and a single curving line in the green "leaf" strip.

CURVED-SEAM BLOCKS

FIG 16

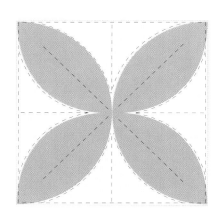

This type of block often has a very strong graphic identity of its own that is difficult to override or ignore. Using a straight-line quilting treatment either in the background spaces or within the shapes themselves will, of course, make an excellent contrast with the curves, but it is interesting to find that curved quilting lines seem to work equally well and can easily add further movement and interest. Straight-line background textures can have the effect of lifting the main curved shapes up and into more prominence. If you want to emphasise the overall outline of the curved main shape, echo quilting is always a good and appropriate choice – just think of the striking appearance of Hawaiian appliqué quilts – which is easy to mark and equally easy to quilt, either by hand or machine.

▼► FIG 16   The smooth shallow curves of the Orange Peel block can be divided up with contrasting straight lines or echoed. Echoing the main shapes and adding straight lines to the background will give a more formal look to the block, while adding curved lines to both the shapes and the background will give an even spread of texture that could be developed into simple motifs within the main shapes.

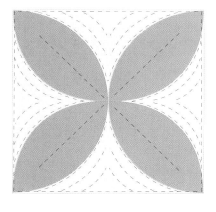
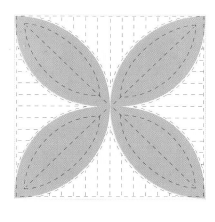
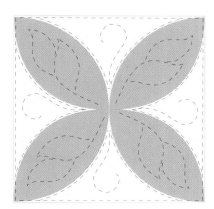

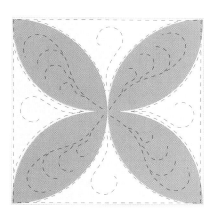

FIG 17

FIG 18

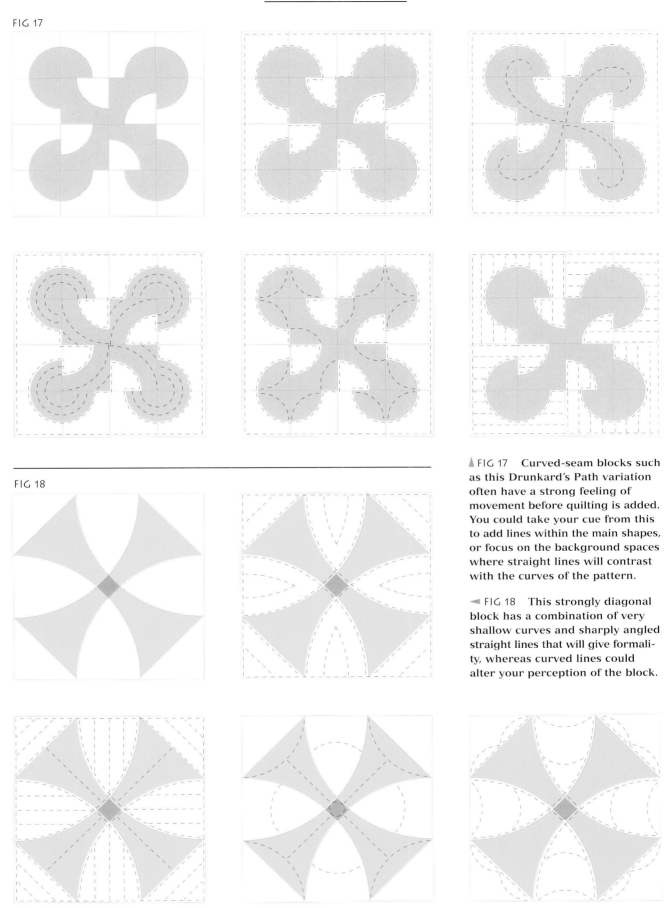

▲ FIG 17 Curved-seam blocks such as this Drunkard's Path variation often have a strong feeling of movement before quilting is added. You could take your cue from this to add lines within the main shapes, or focus on the background spaces where straight lines will contrast with the curves of the pattern.

◀ FIG 18 This strongly diagonal block has a combination of very shallow curves and sharply angled straight lines that will give formality, whereas curved lines could alter your perception of the block.

FIG 19

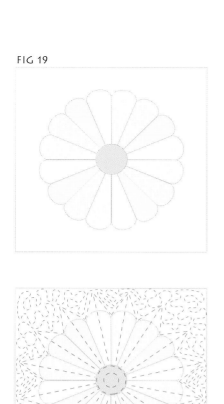

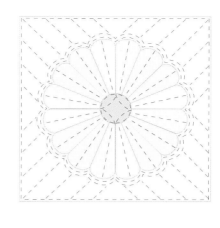

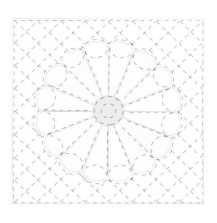

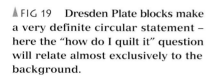

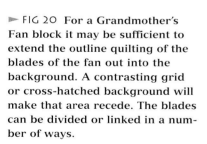

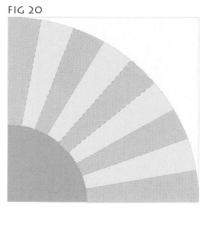

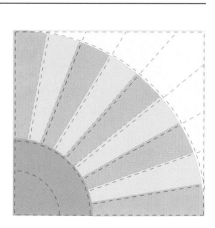

▲ FIG 19   Dresden Plate blocks make a very definite circular statement – here the "how do I quilt it" question will relate almost exclusively to the background.

► FIG 20   For a Grandmother's Fan block it may be sufficient to extend the outline quilting of the blades of the fan out into the background. A contrasting grid or cross-hatched background will make that area recede. The blades can be divided or linked in a number of ways.

FIG 20

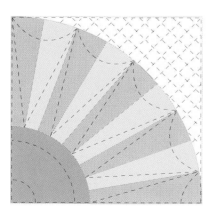

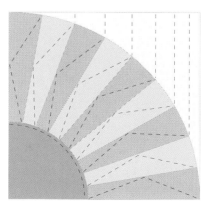

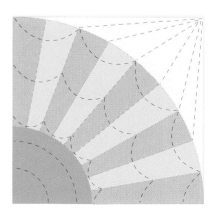

Double Wedding Ring quilt made by Shirley Prescott. Outline, crosshatch and simple motif quilting have been combined very effectively in this piece.

FIG 21

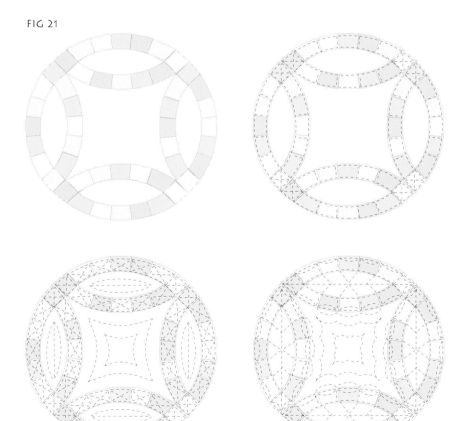

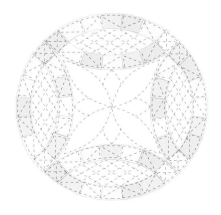

◄ FIG 21 A single circle of Double Wedding Ring is as attractive as a full-sized quilt. In either case, the open areas available for quilting are relatively small, but demanding of attention in their own right, and basic outline quilting often looks insufficient. Echo quilting gives a very strong emphasis to the background shapes, while developing a motif for the central area and adding contrasting straight-line texture in the "melons" puts more focus on the centre.

APPLIQUÉ BLOCKS

The choices of how to quilt an appliqué block tend to focus more on background textures and character quilting to add extra detail and realism to the appliqué shapes. As with pieced blocks, outline quilting of the overall shape formed by the appliqué pattern is almost always essential for good definition before any further texture is added.

By the very nature of the appliqué technique, there is no design grid as there would be in a pieced block so you will rely more heavily on the cues and clues to be found within the fabrics and the overall "look" of the design when considering your options and choices to decide how to quilt it. Is the pattern itself traditional or contemporary, symmetrical or non-symmetrical? Is there some particular area you want to emphasise? Or perhaps a particular shape you could adapt and use as part of a quilting pattern?

Straight lines are always an excellent contrast to the curved shapes that often feature in appliqué, which explains why crosshatching or gridding is so familiar on appliqué quilts whether they were made yesterday or yesteryear, but this does not preclude the use of curved lines.

Basic and uncomplicated backgrounds, grids or crosshatching, or just diagonal parallel lines, often work well, as does very closely spaced quilting, such as vermicelli or meander quilting. Both can be done by hand or machine, although meander quilting is perhaps more suited to machine work.

Strong graphic shapes are always a good subject for echo quilting. Working the echo quilting very closely (with the lines almost touching each other) can give a heavily textured traditional look that is highly effective.

You may have worked the appliqué using fusible web; this makes it difficult (if not impossible) to quilt within the applied shapes, so you will need to take care not to overquilt the background, or the finished piece may look unbalanced.

FIG 22

◄ ▲ FIG 22   A good proportion of background space and a non-symmetrical central design is not perhaps the description you would expect for the perennially popular Sunbonnet Sue block. This might be a good place to practise meander quilting to fill the space, or you might prefer to go a step further and consider background quilting that has a slightly quirky or random feel to it, such as the continuous loop daisies or the individual stars shown here.

FIG 23

► FIG 23 Outline quilting adds emphasis to the strong shape of this traditional-look Turkey Tracks appliqué block. There is a large central appliqué shape which could have straight or curved lines added to it for extra texture and interest, while closely spaced straight lines in the background contrast with the curved appliqué shapes.

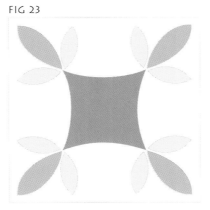
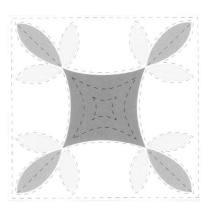
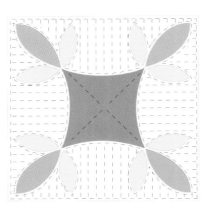
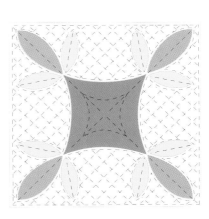

FIG 24

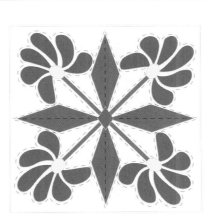

◄ FIG 24 Quilting around the main outlines may be sufficient for an appliqué block where the shapes fill most of the block area. Adding diagonal parallel straight lines in the background reflects the diagonal placement of the flowers.

➤ FIG 25 A "closed" appliqué
pattern such as this simple wreath
is a very strong pattern and shape
that leaves very little background
space. The main interest, apart
from outlining the wreath, will lie
naturally in the centre space,
which can be filled with diagonal
or straight lines, or a motif of
your choosing.

FIG 25

*Variations on a theme – two Rose Wreath appliqué
blocks with straight-line background quilting. Machine
quilting calls for precision and accuracy – two qualities
not evident in the centre of the left-hand block!*

FIG 26

◄ FIG 26 Outlining this wreath and perhaps adding a few lines to the four flowers may be sufficient to balance a basic grid or cross-hatch in the central space, or you may want to consider suggesting an additional simple shape at the centre which could be filled with texture.

▼ FIG 27   This Oak Leaf and Reel appliqué block has a central shape with a closed area surrounding it – this gives you an opportunity to use different types and scales of background quilting in addition to the initial outlining and perhaps a few "character" lines. Echo quilt-ing will give a dense texture to the outer background, or straight lines can be arranged so that they reflect the diagonal nature of the leaf placement.

FIG 27

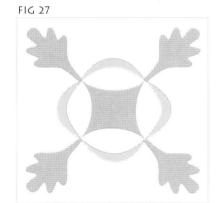
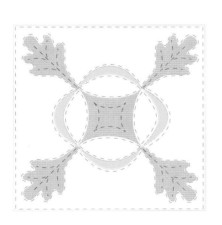
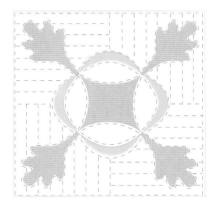

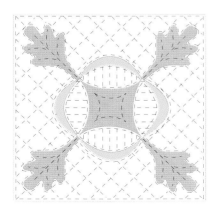
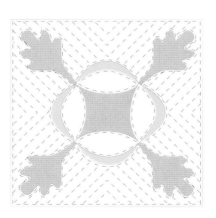

STRIP-PIECED BLOCKS

Any block that has been made by, or includes, strip piecing will have many seams to consider. Strip piecing, where fabric strips are measured, cut and joined into "new" fabric, usually has the majority of seams lying in the same direction, something to be borne in mind when planning outline quilting. You can work with the main design grid of the block rather than individual strips, or consider adding movement with a mixture of curved and straight lines.

▶ FIG 28 Working within and across the main seam lines of a strip-pieced block such as this Rail Fence opens up a number of possibilities which are easy to draft and mark.

FIG 28

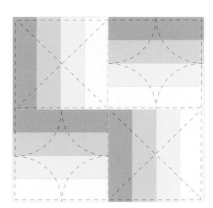
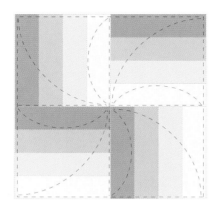
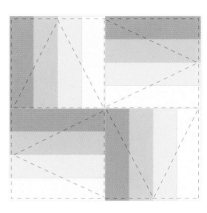

FIG 29

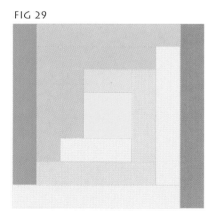
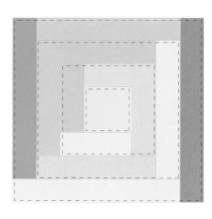

◀ FIG 29 Outline quilting along each seam of a Log Cabin block is effective but it takes a lot of time for a little effect. Consider using short straight or curved lines across the seams based on the halving principle as alternatives.

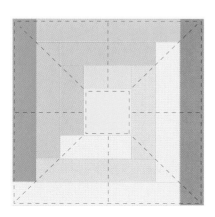
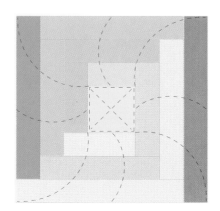
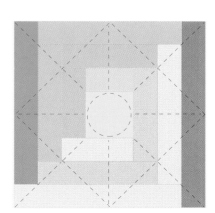

FIG 30

◄ FIG 30   Just changing the direction of the diagonal lines for the background of a Roman Stripe block can give it more balance; experimenting with the halving principle using curved lines may help you to develop a pleasingly simple motif to fill the large triangle of background space.

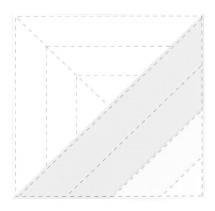

▼ FIG 31   Once you have done the outline quilting on a Mariner's Compass block it seems that there is very little else to be done and very little space in which to do it. Halving the spaces between the points of the compass with straight lines complements the look of the block but you can see how easy it is to overdo this and have a jumbled looking arrangement of straight lines. Using short curved lines to connect up and outline the points is simple but effective.

FOUNDATION-PIECED BLOCKS

FIG 31

Foundation, or paper piecing as it is often called, is a popular technique which helps you achieve complex patterns, razor sharp points and stunning precision. This is done by stitching from the reverse side along lines drawn or stamped onto a paper or muslin foundation. A paper foundation can be torn away when the stitching is completed, but if muslin or lightweight interlining foundation has been used, there will be an extra layer in addition to seam allowances, and a foundation-pieced block or quilt top may be a better candidate for quilting by machine than by hand.

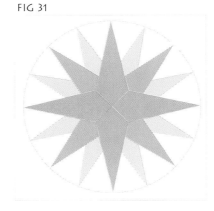

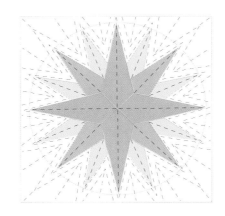

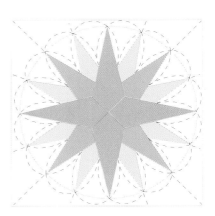

COMBINING BLOCKS

FOUR BLOCKS

Fascinating things happen the minute you put four identical blocks together. Not only does it create a new, bigger and more interesting block, but secondary patterns and spaces may be made at the centre which can change and enhance the impact of the original block.

Treating each of the four blocks as a single repeating unit rather than part of a new whole can work well and may give a satisfactory resolution of the centre space. However, it is often worth taking a few moments to focus on this area to see just what the possibilities may be. There may be a printed pattern or stencil that is absolutely right for this new centre space in terms of both fit and style, which means that all you have to do is transfer that pattern onto the fabric. If this is the case, spend a little time thinking about what you will quilt on the remaining surface. Perhaps you could adapt part of this pattern to fit into some of the background or corner spaces. Alternatively you could use the halving principle and the seam lines as a guide to developing some simple but effective quilting treatments of your own.

Depending on the effect produced by putting four particular blocks together, you may feel that it is as important to emphasise the corner areas as the centre. An easy-to-do method of achieving this emphasis is to have radiating lines at each corner fanning either towards or away from the centre of the piece. Alternatively you could close off the corners with a curved line or angled parallel lines.

Viewing the four blocks from a distance or through a reducing glass may help you to form an impression of which elements or shapes you feel are most suitable to emphasise and draw attention to.

You might want to plan the quilting so that there will be lines linking up and moving between the blocks and/or helping to create the illusion of an additional outer frame. This can help to add a further subtle emphasis to the central space.

Rather than work with the new unit of four blocks together, try working with a drawing of a single block and make an asymmetrical quilting plan for it so when four blocks are put together a secondary pattern is automatically created at the centre.

Putting four blocks together means you will be working on a smaller scale than that of a full size quilt. Since the finished project is therefore more likely to be a "look at" piece or wallhanging, you may find you are prepared to do more intricate, detailed and closely spaced quilting, either by hand or machine, perhaps taking some of your inspiration for a quilting design from the fabrics used or from the overall style of the piece as described earlier.

Any border that frames and completes a four-block wallhanging or small quilt is a very important part of the finished piece and deserves some consideration in that context. If you have definite ideas for using a specific pattern or type of pattern in the border, take a little time to audition it first before marking it onto the fabric, making sure it fits the space and works well with any other quilting patterns and texture you plan to include. Guidelines and ideas for borders appear in a later section.

Even the best-laid and stitched plans can go awry and it could be that the quilting needs to take into account an unexpected fullness at the centre where a number of seams meet. In any event you will also need to think about the number of seam allowances to be quilted through or avoided – it may prove simpler to work across and over them rather than along them.

What is "enough" quilting? This small wallhanging would definitely benefit from additional quilting in the cream background spaces as well as within the main areas of the four star blocks themselves. The straight-line echo quilting in the centre is quite effective, as is the squares-on-point border pattern, which is based on the spacing of the block seam lines, but the overall spread of quilted texture could be significantly improved with just a little more care.

FIG 32

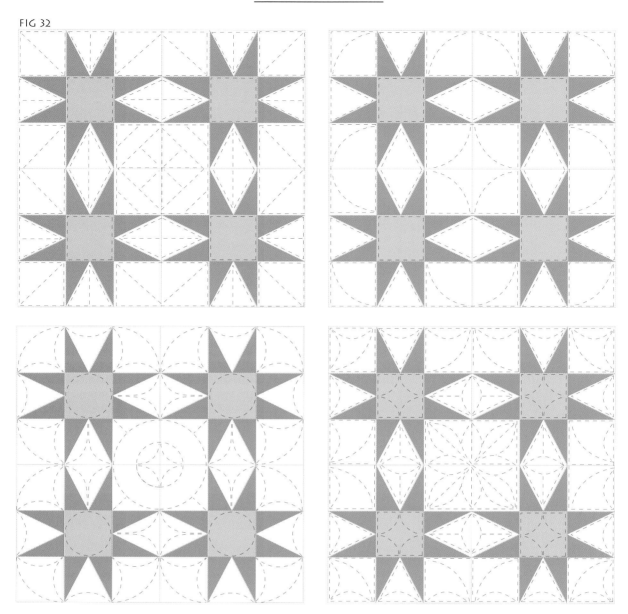

▲ FIG 32 Putting four blocks together may produce a large plain square at the centre. Using the halving principle with either curved or straight lines it is possible to develop a number of quilting solutions, all of which are easy to mark and stitch.

➤ FIG 33 Outline quilting and a straightforward grid in all the background areas does not work well when just four blocks are put together. Although the straight lines provide good contrast with the curved piecing, the overall effect is lacklustre. Look instead for ways of echoing some or all of the new shapes created by this setting, using straight lines to divide up the shapes or fill them with straight-line texture that has several changes of direction.

FIG 33

FIG 34

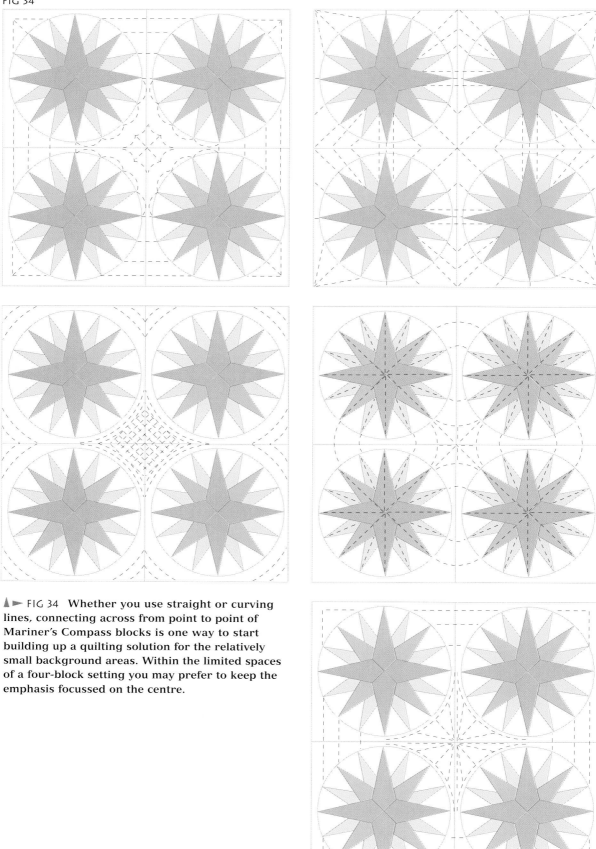

▲ ► FIG 34 Whether you use straight or curving lines, connecting across from point to point of Mariner's Compass blocks is one way to start building up a quilting solution for the relatively small background areas. Within the limited spaces of a four-block setting you may prefer to keep the emphasis focussed on the centre.

FIG 35

FIG 36

▲ FIG 35 The new centre square created by putting four Basket blocks together is relatively small – simply outlining and echoing the four small triangles or the complete square may give enough emphasis to this space or you could develop a curved line motif which will contrast with all the short straight lines of the piecing.

◄ FIG 36 Careful placement of quilting lines can suggest a central focus even if there is none.

FIG 37

FIG 38

Busy prints call for simple quilting – this small star quilt is machine quilted using only straight lines that echo a seam line or halve a space. Notice the effect of the quilted square at the centre of each star.

◄ FIG 37   Straight lines dividing up the area of the larger triangles add directional texture to the centre and background, but the contrast of curving lines may add more emphasis to the Square within a Square blocks both at the centre and the edges and corners.

▼ FIG 38   Straight lines only, or a combination of straight and curved, based on the halving principle produce a number of quilting solutions by emphasising different areas of the new large block.

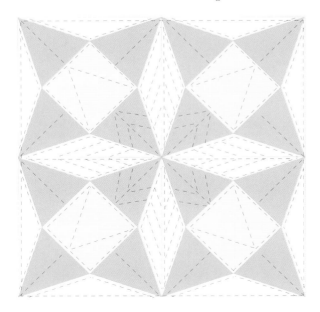

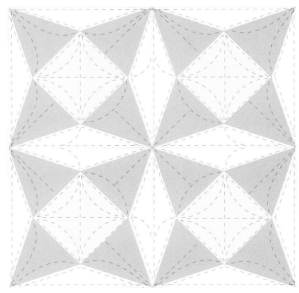

FIG 39

FIG 40

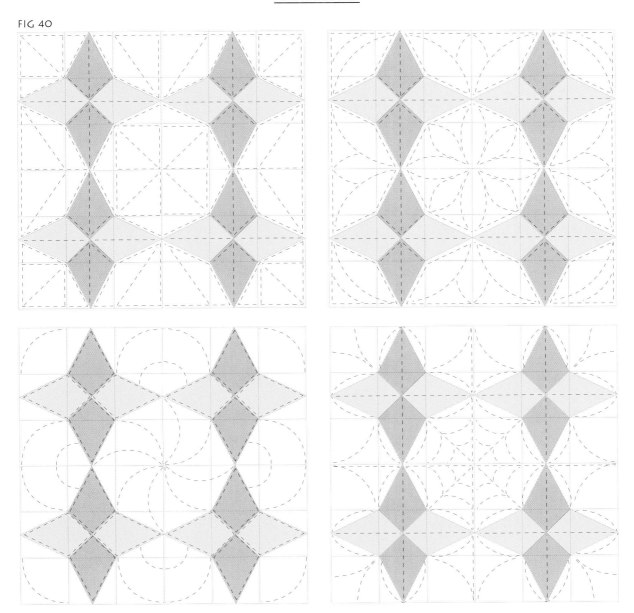

◄ FIG 39   Putting four strongly directional blocks, such as this Palm block, together may give a new block with no empty centre space. Instead you will probably be more concerned with how to enhance the new pieced shape - from outline quilting to close meander quilting, there are a number of ways to achieve this.

▲ FIG 40   Outline quilting and a little halving does not enhance the attractive centre shape although it gives an even spread of texture. Experimenting with a mixture of curved and straight lines may produce a more pleasing result.

FULL QUILT, BLOCKS SET EDGE TO EDGE

As we saw earlier, setting just four blocks together offers the challenge of a new central space for quilting. When a full-sized quilt is made by setting identical blocks together edge to edge, the challenge becomes even greater, with "new" spaces galore and a very large total area to quilt. This edge-to-edge repeating setting is one of the most popular in the quilting lexicon, which means that you are not the first to become glassy-eyed at the quilting prospect before you! You will probably want to look for quilting ideas that will enhance the blocks and give an even spread of texture across the quilt. Your preferences for hand or machine quilting may influence the type of pattern you choose, not forgetting the amount of quilting time you have available and any deadlines for completion of the project. There will be cues and clues for you to consider in the type of block, fabrics used, colours chosen and the overall style of the quilt before you look at just some of the possibilities that could be developed using the halving principle with some easy straight and curved lines. Remember that you don't need to have the complete or final quilting solution totally resolved before you begin quilting – do that vital outlining first while you think about the rest.

Star patterns are perennial favourites. The Spinning Star blocks (left) are quilted (as on page 46). The irregular foundation pieced stars (right) have a similar simple quilting solution, but in this case more emphasis could be quilted into the space at the centre of the quilt. The telltale puffy look indicates that a closer overall density of quilting would not go amiss.

FIG 41

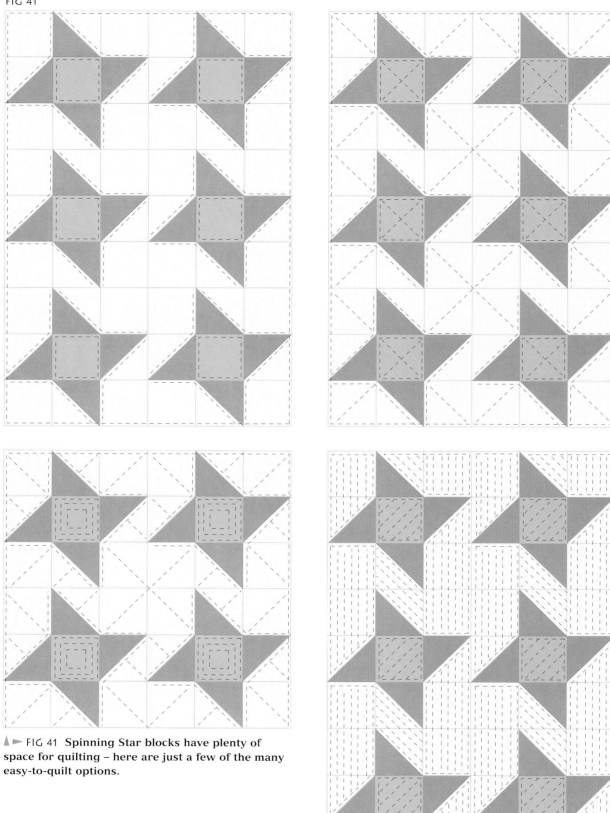

▲ ► FIG 41 Spinning Star blocks have plenty of space for quilting – here are just a few of the many easy-to-quilt options.

45

FIG 41 (CONT.)

FIG 42

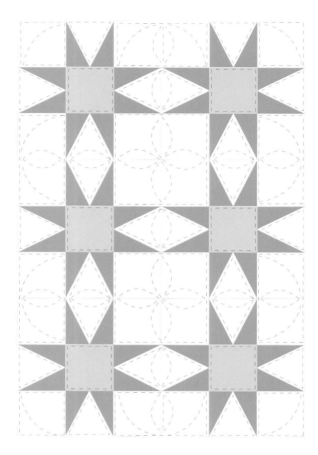

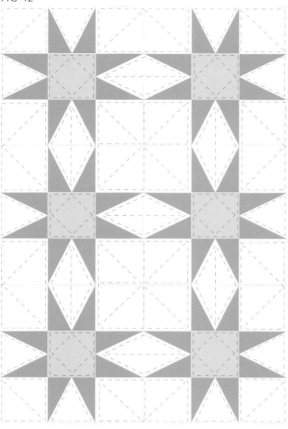

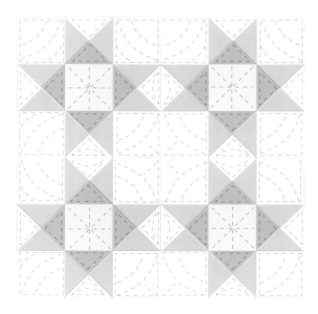

▲ FIG 42 Beginning to build up quilting solutions by halving the spaces with straight or curved lines.

◀▼ FIG 43 Here the background spaces between the Ohio Star blocks have an even balance and spread of quilting using either straight or curved lines.

FIG 43

FIG 44

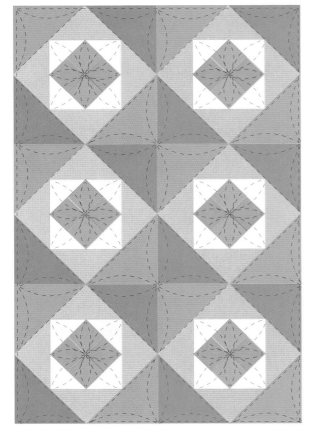

◄ ▲ ► FIG 44 Beginning with basic outline quilting you can go on to develop any number of easy-to-stitch ideas using the simplest of straight or curved lines – on this page and overleaf the emphasis is on some of the curved line possibilities and their variations.

FIG 45 (PAGE 51)   Where there is a large proportion of background space such as in this Four Point Star block, using the halving principle can help you to develop some solutions which will fill space quickly and effectively whilst maintaining that all-important even spread of texture.

FIG 46 (PAGE 52)   In this block there is very little background space, the main focus being on the large diagonal star points and the centre square. Your quilting solutions could again be based on the halving principle using straight or curved lines in addition to basic outline quilting, but you will almost certainly want to place some quilting within the star points to maintain an even texture.

FIG 44 (CONT.)

FIG 45

FIG 46

FIG 47

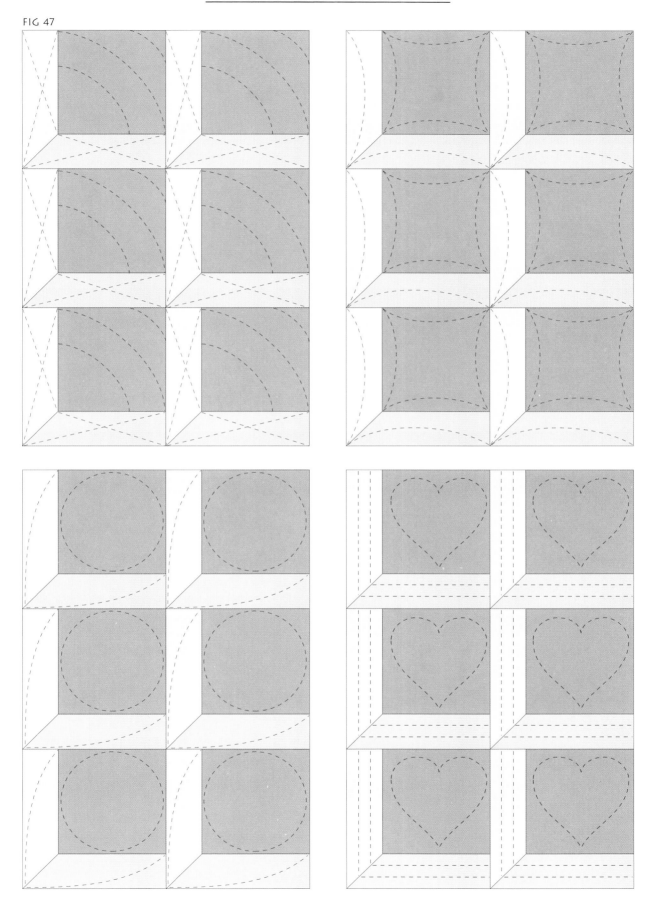

FIG 48

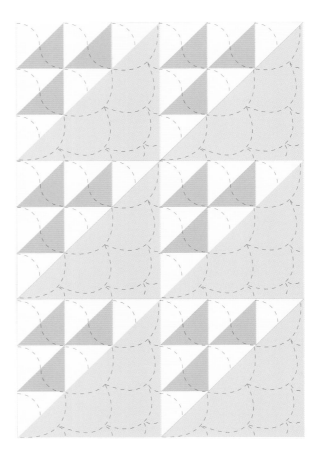

◄▲ FIG 48   A block divided diagonally can sometimes have the appearance of being out of balance
when it is repeated. All of the suggestions illustrated
here are based on the halving principle and follow
cues from the actual piecing or construction of the
block. Working with the skeleton of the blocks in
this way is easy to do and also allows you to mark
a little and then stitch a little, rather than marking
up a full quilt top first, which can be a major under-
taking.

FIG 47 (PAGE 53)   The strong 3-D element of Attic
Windows is difficult to ignore, particularly if you
are dealing with high contrast of fabric colours or
tones. It is the "window" area of the large square
that demands attention – if it is a plain fabric, whatever texture is stitched here will show to good
effect whereas an important or interesting print
will obscure the finer points of any detailed motif.
You may find that your quilting solutions are more
successful if you consider the possibilities of using
minimal quilting and the simplest of lines first for
the "frames" of the windows - none of the options
presented on page 53 is perfect but they do indicate
some of the different starting points.

FIG 49

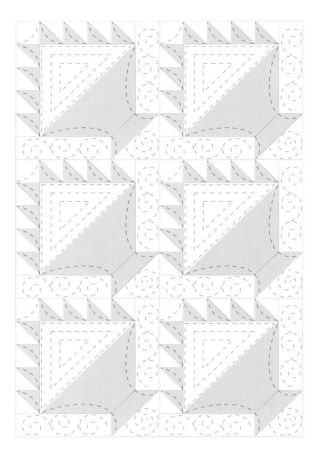

▲ FIG 49   The traditional Basket block set edge to edge leaves only a narrow strip of background space for quilting – the largest areas are within the basket "handle" and the base of the basket itself. Notice how effectively a simple scrolling pattern fills the small background area.

► FIG 50 A visually complex pattern such as Storm at Sea can present choices of different areas to highlight – look carefully at the placement of the red dashed lines in the following figures. You may choose to emphasise specific areas by making other areas recede through the use of closely spaced quilting – although not illustrated here, the main shapes of this pattern can appear more dominant if close meander quilting is used for the small background spaces.

FIG 51 (PAGE 58/9)   "Awkward" background spaces are a feature of many appliqué blocks! This is probably why crosshatching and echo quilting are such popular choices for quilting solutions in this type of quilt. From the illustrations overleaf you can see the development of very basic quilted detail within the appliqué shapes, followed by a variety of suggestions (some more appealing than others) for quilting the background.

FIG 50

FIG 51

FIG 52

▼► FIG 52 Double Wedding Ring is an attractive
and highly graphic quilt with large areas that need
texture. Halving spaces with straight lines or echo
quilting will give an even spread of texture; straight
lines will contrast with the curves or you may prefer
to focus on the centre spaces and use a simple motif.
Notice the subtle differences in the "melon" shapes
in the three figures that feature crosshatching or
gridding.

FIG 53

▼► FIG 53 Virtually all of the Drunkard's Path variations, only one of which is illustrated here, have very dominant curving main pattern lines. As in the case of some appliqué blocks, it may be easier to focus on quilting an overall texture, such as a grid or simple straight lines, in the background spaces. Echo quilting might be very effective and equally easy to mark and quilt, or you might want to explore the possibility of freehand swirls and spirals.

FIG 54

◄▼FIG 54 Mariner's Compass blocks, as we have already seen, have relatively little background space to fill with quilting. Simply echoing the new shape created by joining blocks together, or beginning to halve spaces by connecting up the compass points from block to block, will give you two starting points for reviewing quilting possibilities. Remember that a block such as this has the disadvantage of numerous seam allowances – it may be more viable to consider quilting down the centre of each of the compass points than to outline them.

FULL QUILT USING TWO BLOCKS

Two different simple pieced blocks in an alternating set can make a very striking quilt with a traditional look, and the "how do I quilt it?" question becomes a more interesting challenge to resolve. Basic outline quilting on its own can leave relatively large spaces not only unquilted but looking somewhat forlorn. It may not be necessary to spend endless hours staring at these spaces and wondering where you will find just the right pattern to fill them. If you work the outline quilting first, you may find that you get a better feel for what additional quilting would look pleasing as you are stitching. Think about using the halving principle and the cues and clues already in the quilt either in the overall "look" of the piece, or the skeleton of seam lines contained within the individual blocks as a guide and starting point for adding a few simple lines and building up gradually rather than trying to make all your design decisions at once. Do you want to highlight or feature one block more than the other or do you want the blocks to blend together as much as possible? What would happen if you filled in all of the background space with a single texture such as meander or gridding? Could you use two or three different background textures in different parts of the quilt? What are the possibilities for using echo quilting around the main outlines of both blocks? If any one shape is commonly shared by both blocks, for example both have a centre square, you might want to think about filling all such shapes in the same way, which will have a subtly unifying effect.

Think about using the halving principle as one means of beginning to divide up the spaces between and around the blocks and see what scope there is for developing this further, perhaps using a combination of straight and curving lines. Are there any spaces which seem ideally suited to being filled by a simple motif? What about the cues and clues already in the quilt top – prints, plains, predominant colour, overall style? You might also look at the skeleton of seam lines contained within the individual blocks and use this as a starting point, adding some straight or curved lines within the block shapes. As we have already agreed, it is not essential to arrive at a complete quilting solution in one confident leap, and building up gradually by a series of small steps instead of trying to make all your design decisions at once is a more flexible approach which can give excellent results.

Small quilts require precision piecing. Scribble, meander or vermicelli quilting is easy to do on a sewing machine with the feed dogs dropped, but it takes practice to do it well – notice the small areas of extra fullness. Nonetheless, close background texture contrasts well with the main pieced blocks, and the holly leaves quilted in the border add a final festive touch. Border quilted by Sally Radway.

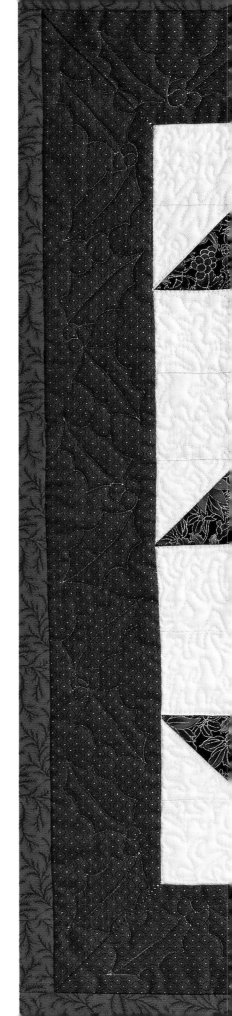

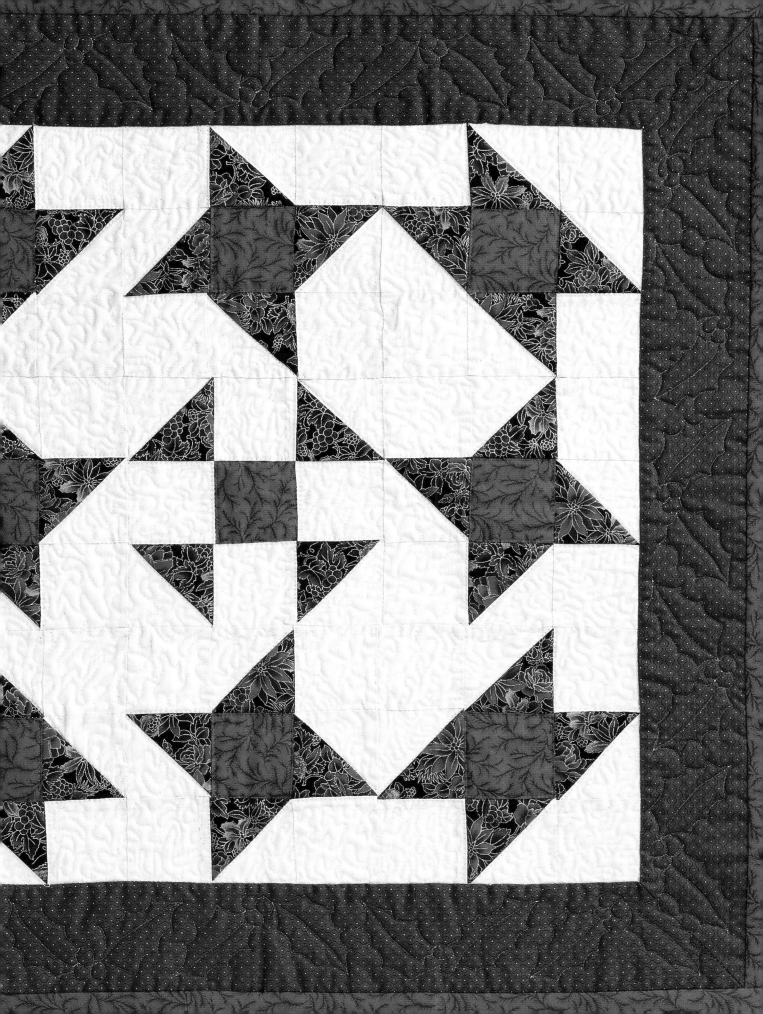

FIG 55

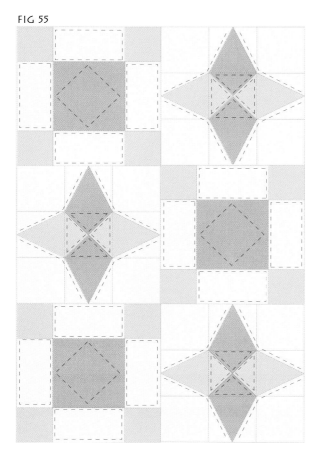

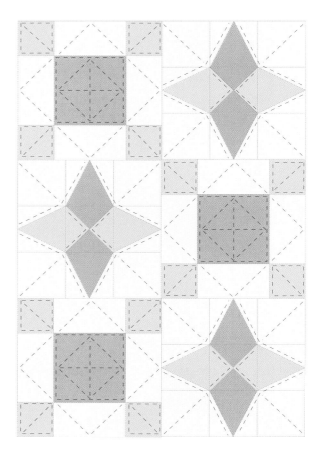

◄▲► FIG 55 Experiment with using the design grid of the individual blocks and the main seam lines as well as the halving principle. All of the possibilities illustrated here would be easy to mark and stitch and could be developed further if you wished – you might try mixing straight and curved lines and see what happens.

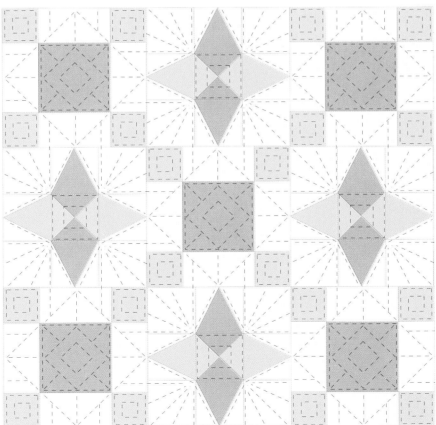

FIG 56

▲ FIG 56A   An eight-pointed star combines with a four-pointed star leaving plenty of background space to be filled. You could start reviewing your quilting options by halving the spaces with diagonal straight lines. These lines do not necessarily have to feature in the final quilting plan but might help you look at the spaces between the blocks and consider how they could be further sub-divided and developed. From this starting point it would be easy to make a spider's-web pattern within each of the large background squares – this pattern could perhaps be repeated at the centre of each of the main blocks, or at the centre of the eight-pointed stars alone.

▲ FIG 56B   You may want to highlight or feature one block more than the other – here's a starting point for doing just that. The four-pointed star block has the suggestion of echo quilting which gives a subtle but defined emphasis. You could build on this emphasis by additional straight lines of echo quilting both inside the block and between the two lines illustrated here. Working from this, consider what other additions you might choose to make.

FIG 57

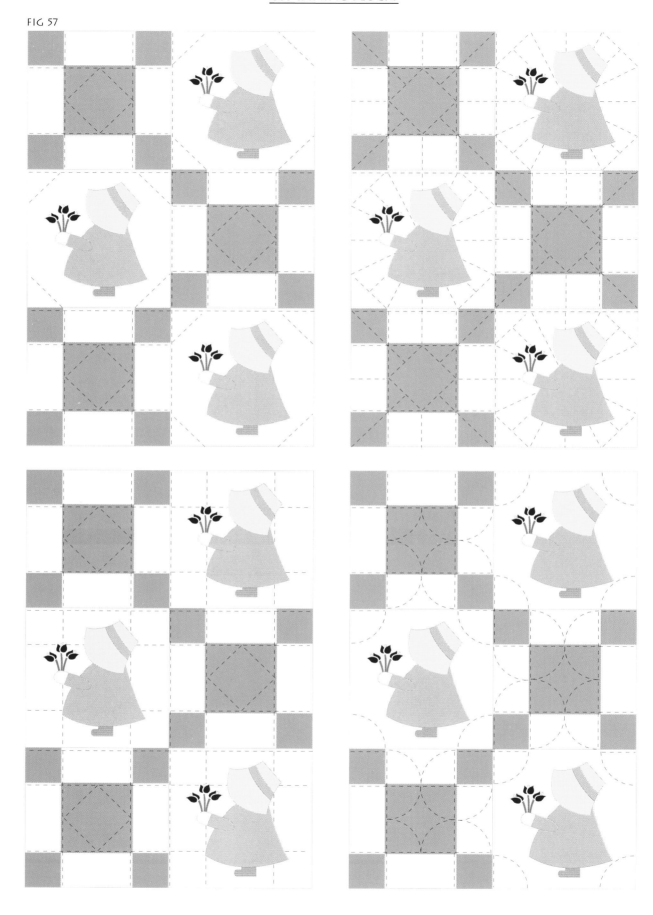

FIG 58

◄ FIG 57   Alternating pieced and appliqué blocks can be great fun, whether you use very simple blocks, such as the two illustrated here, or two that are more complex and detailed. Again, basic outline quilting is an excellent starting point for simple quilting options and you might want to look back to the section on single blocks (p12) for additional possibilities.

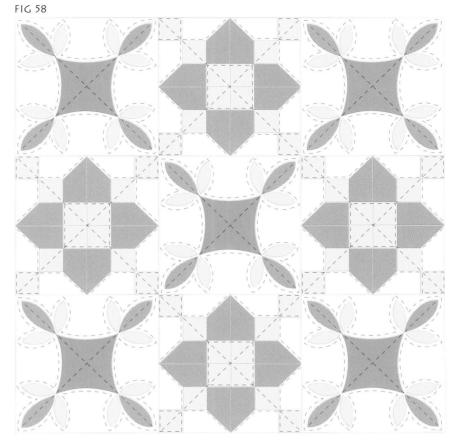

▲ FIG 58   A deceptively simple two-block quilt with a festive air! Some very basic outline quilting has been suggested in this illustration plus straight diagonal lines linking the pieced blocks to each other. Notice too the crossing diagonal lines at the centre of both blocks which adds a little continuity. From here a number of solutions are possible and I'm sure that by now you are familiar with some of them! For instance you could fill in the background space between the appliqué and pieced edges with a regular grid or meander quilting – this would increase the emphasis on the appliqué block by making that background area recede.

MAIN BLOCK AND PLAIN BLOCK

If you have eked out just a few pieced or appliqué blocks and made them go further than you thought possible by the careful addition of plain or spacer blocks, you may ultimately find yourself wondering what to quilt in "all that space". This type of quilt setting puts almost as much emphasis on the spaces as on the blocks themselves. Faced with this type of dilemma, most of us would trot off in search of a pattern that looked just right and was also exactly the correct size to fit the space. Of course there is no reason why you should not find a suitable motif that fits the space and works well, but try to avoid using a motif that leaves a lot of unquilted space around it. For example, a nine-inch feather wreath set in the middle of a twelve- or fourteen-inch square would look less than satisfactory.

Use the halving principle to help you start making decisions. Just subdividing a particular area into halves and then quarters may give you some ideas about arranging motifs to fit the space, or you can use these initial divisions to develop your own pattern. If you need some start-up help and ideas for this, perhaps looking through some of the patterns on page 176 will point up just a few of the numerous possibilities that are waiting to be discovered.

Main and plain is a frequently used and traditional setting for appliqué blocks because it highlights the block design so well. Of course, the reason it highlights the block design is the amount of space it leaves for quilting, which is great if you know exactly what you are going to quilt in that space, but not so great if you don't. The other reason this is a popular setting is that it means twice the area for half the work in terms of piecing or appliqué – why make sixteen identical blocks if you can get by with only eight? This always seems like a good idea when making the sixth or seventh block, when it is all too easy to overlook the quilting questions that this setting will ultimately pose. Just because there is "all that space" for quilting does not necessarily mean that it has to be filled with complicated designs or motifs – one effective and rather subtle solution might be to repeat the main outline and shapes of the pieced or appliqué pattern in the main block. Background textures such as gridding or meandering can also look good if attention is given to scale – remember the even spread of texture you are aiming for. And I'm sure you haven't forgotten about the all-important role of the not-so-visible outline quilting! Whilst you are doing this essential stitching, think about the scope for echoing the main pattern lines and continuing to echo right up to the midpoint of the plain block.

The quilt opposite has just started on a long journey – from imperfectly pieced nine-patch blocks hastily set together in a main and plain format to an unknown final destination! Quilted texture is obviously going to show far more clearly in the large open spaces than on the printed fabrics, and the shape of the open or background spaces will need to be taken into account.

The first step of the journey should be outline quilting around all the main pieced squares to give some basic definition, then crossing diagonal lines dividing the main shapes might look effective – you can see that an experimental line or two has been stitched in the top right-hand corner to try this out. It would be useful to spend a little time trying out some of the possibilities based on the halving principle or connecting up various pattern seams, perhaps using a mixture of straight and curved lines. If you are willing to postpone your quilting decisions for a little while longer, you may find inspiration from folding and cutting paper. This is an excellent way of producing "personalised" motifs that will put your own particular stamp on a quilt – begin with very simple shapes such as the four shown and experiment with various arrangements of lines within the basic shape. It would also be fun to play around with a number of simple cut paper shapes such as hearts and leaves and see how many different composite patterns you can devise – you may be pleasantly surprised at your creative skills!

The open spaces of the plain blocks on this nine-patch quilt are perfect for filling with texture. You can use simple cut paper shapes such as the four pictured above to help you begin making choices for quilting motifs. "Auditioning" motif styles in this way is often easier than looking through pattern books and trying to envisage the final effect.

FIG 59

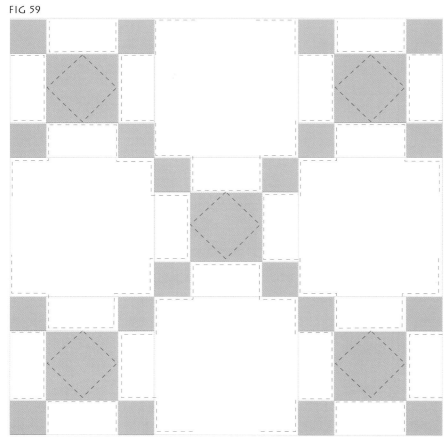

◄ ▼ ► FIG 59   Beginning with outline quilting of the main block it is possible to develop a straight line treatment which frames a space in the plain block or a simple motif that fills the same space. Curved line treatments might be equally effective at filling space. You may find a quilting pattern or adapt an appliqué pattern for the plain space – in the illustration overleaf, you can see that although the Oak Leaf pattern contrasts well with the straight edges of the piecing, it still leaves a lot of background space. Notice the different quilting in the main nine-patch blocks in all of these examples.

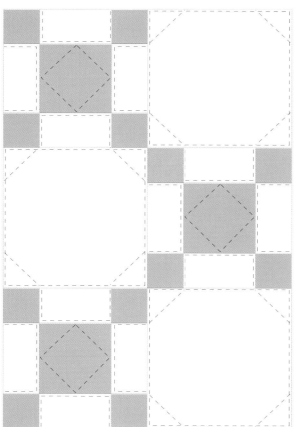

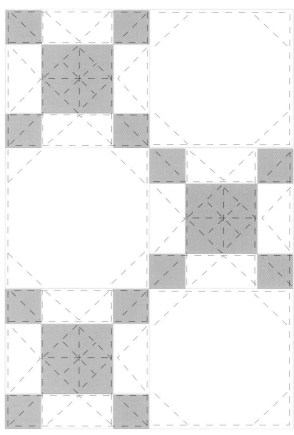

FIG 59 (CONT.)

FIG 60

◀ FIG 60 (PAGE 77)   Four extremely straightforward solutions to filling the plain or spacer blocks with texture – how much quilting is "enough"? Could you develop either of the curved line suggestions further?

FIG 61

▼▶ FIG 61   A regular grid or crosshatching may look too flat in the plain blocks; halving the plain spaces with curved lines can be developed into a simple motif that can have echo lines added. Notice how the orientation of the motif can contrast with or repeat that of the main block. Notice also the empty square at the centre of each block – think about adding a contrasting texture or pattern here, or repeating a scaled-down version of the patterns used in the plain blocks.

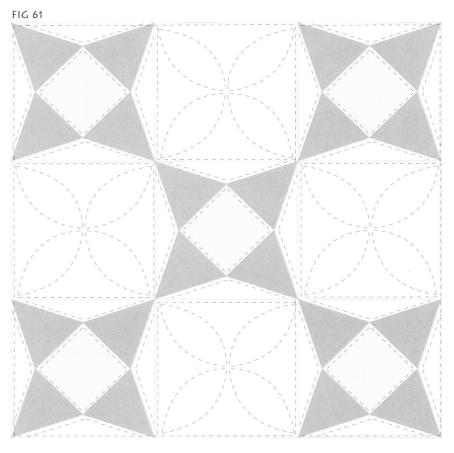

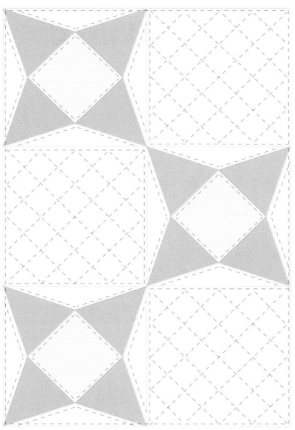

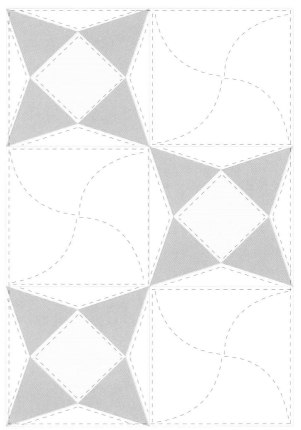

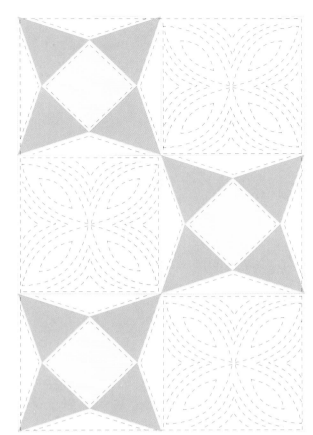

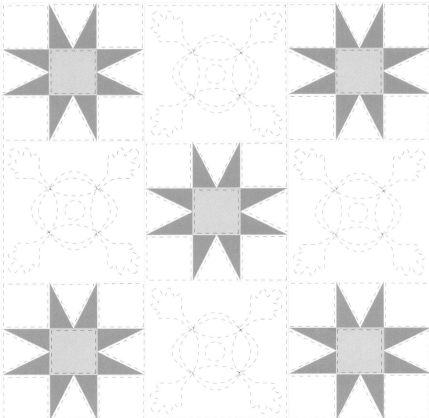

FIG 62

◄ FIG 62   There is a whole host of appliqué patterns that could be easily adapted for quilting patterns – the diagonal orientation of the Oak Leaf and Reel shown here helps to create an impression of unity and helps the eye move across the quilt surface as well as contrasting with the straight edges of the piecing. Single oak leaves could be added in each of the corner squares of the star blocks; alternatively, there is sufficient space to add four more oak leaves to the existing pattern so that they cross the main seam lines.

FIG 63

FIG 64

◄ FIG 63 A selection of predominantly curved line quilting solutions, all of which could be expanded and developed further if necessary – perhaps a spider's web at the centre of the plain block?

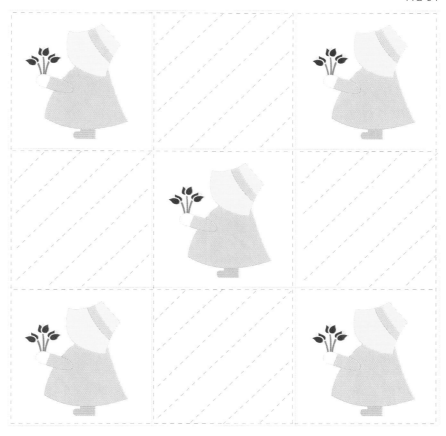

▼ ► FIG 64 Straight line texture in the plain blocks contrasts well with the strong curves of the appliqué, but may appear too rigid. What possibilities could be developed from the curved lines?

FIG 65 (CONT.)

Caution, machine quilting in progress! This example, illustrating part of one of the figures on page 82, shows the clarity of machine-quilted straight lines as well as some of the puckering that may occur if you have been a little lax with your basting technique. The appliqué blocks will certainly require outline quilting, and the main quilting lines already worked will need developing and extending to spread the texture and eliminate most of the unquilted areas. Once a more even spread of texture has been achieved, it might be rewarding to focus on the centres of the quilted stars and emphasise these a little more.

FIG 66

FIG 66 Straight-line textures, curved lines and simple motifs are all reviewed here – form your own opinions as to what is successful and what could be developed. There are more examples overleaf.

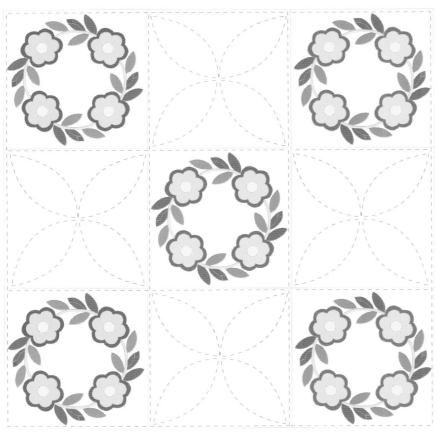

FIG 66 (CONT.)

FIG 67

◄ FIG 67   The lines of this curved block suggest an attractive shape that could be echoed to frame a chosen motif – here you can see treatments which ignore that shape, perhaps to the detriment of the finished piece.

BLOCKS SET ON POINT

Like main and plain, this is a well-tried and tested way of making a few blocks go that little bit further – turn a square on point and it occupies more space (something to do with basic geometry and Pythagoras). Turning blocks on point requires additional and often quite large triangles to fill in the gaps at the corners and edges. Once these triangles have been added, you are then left to contemplate "all that space", which of course leads again to the "how do I quilt it?" question.

Before facing up to the bigger question of how to quilt the blank triangular spaces, you might find it helpful to start by outline quilting all of the main blocks. Keep your focus on these main blocks and look at how you could quilt the remaining spaces there; then you could start to use the halving principle in the larger spaces, using the seam lines of the main blocks as your starting point.

You could consider taking cues from the triangle shapes and running lines or pattern straight along the long outside edges or following the angle of the two shorter inside edges. What about echoing the whole triangle shape, or dividing the triangles in half and echoing each half triangle?

Depending on the style of the quilt blocks and the look you want to achieve, it may be worth considering treating the "fill-in" triangles differently in order to make a strong contrast with the main portion of the quilt. This approach will emphasise the structure of the quilt.

Clever contrasting of straight and curving lines in this quilt made by Sandie Lush. The feather wreaths in the plain blocks have a star at the centre which echoes the pieced star blocks, and the feather theme is continued at the centre of the pieced blocks and also in the border. Notice how effectively the blocks have been textured with straight lines that extend into the sashing strips.

FIG 68

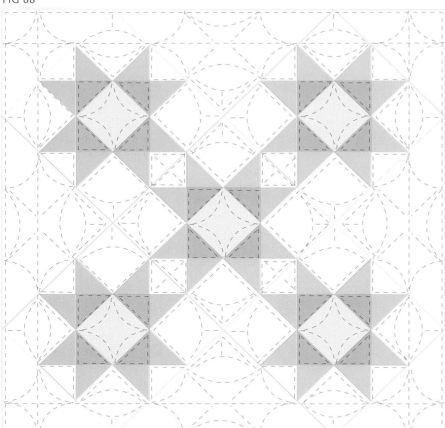

◄ FIG 68A Setting blocks on point not only changes the orientation of the block but produces large triangular spaces. The quilts illustrated here show the difference between an overall spread of texture based on the design grid of the blocks and contrasting texture density in the triangles to suggest a frame for the blocks.

► FIG 68B Working with a framework of curved lines around the edges of the block, fill in the remaining space with parallel straight lines that give a formal "ribbed" look that also contrasts with the more open curving lines.

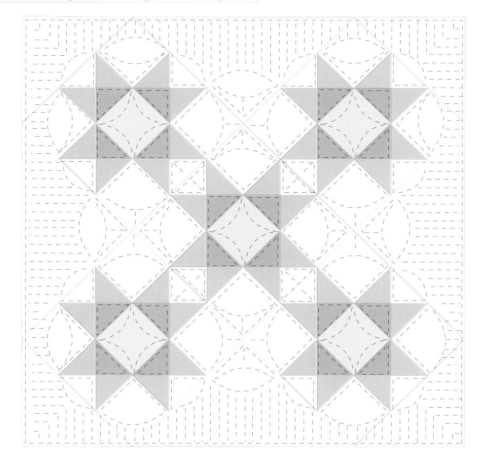

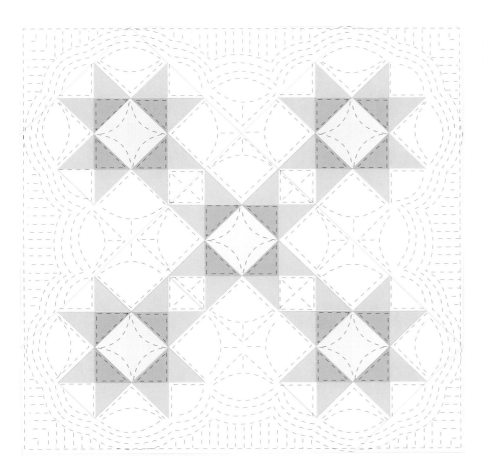

◀ FIG 68C Emphasise the unusual shape created by the curved line frame with three or four lines of echo quilting before filling in with straight lines. If the echo lines were closely spaced, it would be possible to give the impression of cording.

▶ FIG 68D A traditional choice of crosshatch or grid to fill in around the curved frame would give texture to the outer space – but is it sufficiently interesting?

FIG 69

► FIG 69A Blocks set on point with plain blocks in between means even more space to be filled with quilting of some description. A number of different possibilities are shown here, some of which have a more even spread of texture than others; all could be developed further if you use these examples as a starting point.

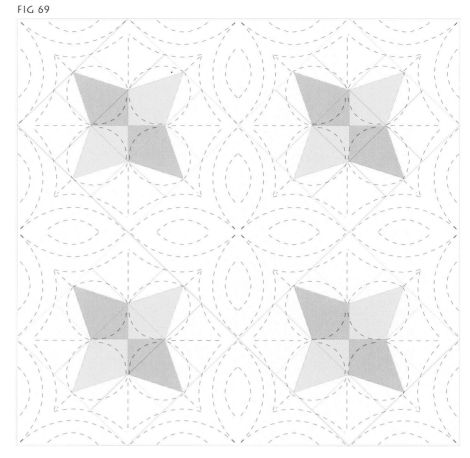

► FIG 69B With this arrangement of simple curved lines in the plain block, a frame is suggested around the main edges of the pieced star block. Would you leave in the "halving" lines shown, or use a different texture inside the frame to highlight the piecing?

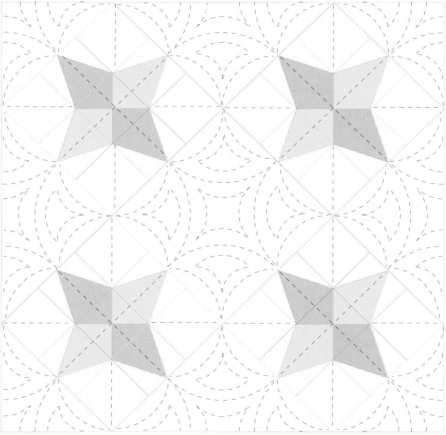

◄ FIG 69C Still framing the pieced block, this time with a circle that touches the four points of the star, consider the effect of echo, meander or grid quilting between the circle and the edges of each of the stars.

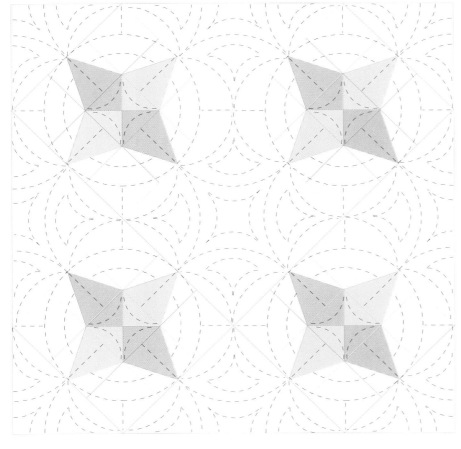

◄ FIG 69D Yet again, the suggestion of a frame around the star, but this time with more feeling of movement derived partly from the circle, which slips behind the star points.

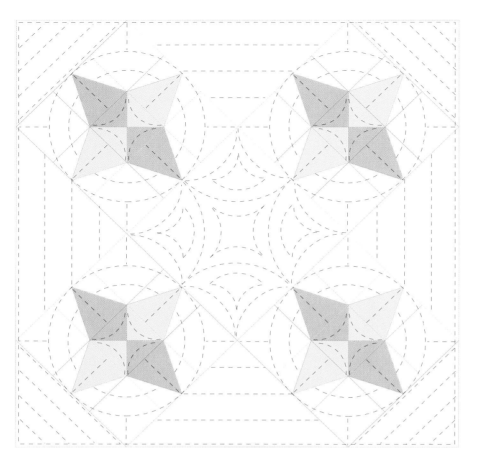

◀ FIG 69E Curved lines contrast with the straight edges of the star in the plain centre square and all remaining space is filled with straight lines running parallel to the quilt edges and angling off at the corners. The width between the parallel lines is determined by connecting the star points and then dividing the remaining space.

► FIG 69F Using a different curved-line motif for the centre, but continuing to keep it simple, this suggestion would need some additions in order to become effective – how would you achieve this?

◄ FIG 69G The scrolls or spirals at each corner of the star blocks give a strong feeling of movement. They also reflect the style of the central motif.

► FIG 69H Emphasis on the shallow angles of the star is added with equally shallow curved lines in the corner squares. Instead of using the parallel straight lines for the outer triangular spaces, it might have been better to experiment with curved lines...

► FIG 69I It is often worthwhile taking a little time to play with some of the variations that are possible and audition them before making any decisions – here a very basic curved-line motif is linked to the surrounding star blocks by continuing the curved lines in each of the outside squares of the blocks.

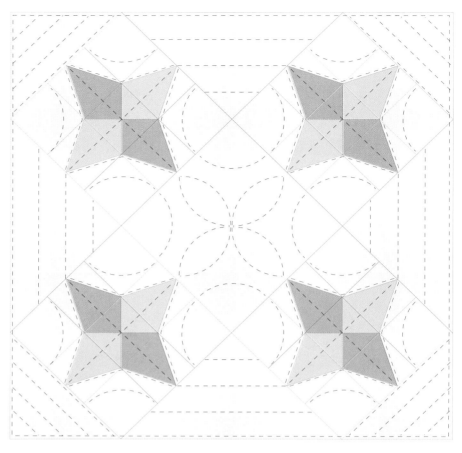

◄ FIG 69J Another twist on the curved central motif theme maintains an even spread of quilting – what substitutions could you make for the straight lines?

► FIG 69K A motif which fills
the whole centre square does not
have to be complicated...

◄ FIG 69L ... and a mixture of
straight and curving lines puts
a slightly different spin on the
centre square!

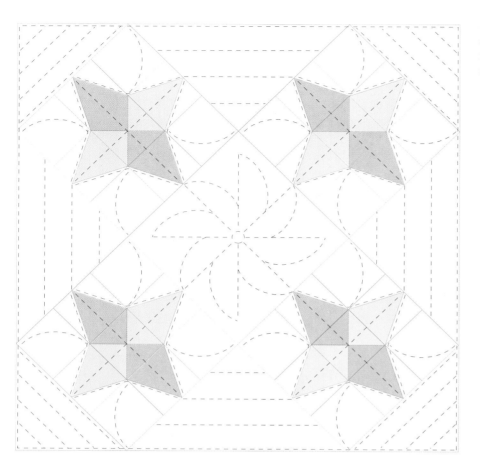

◄ FIG 69M   Use a curve based on the halving principle to connect the star blocks and give some movement...

► FIG 69N   ... or use curves to suggest a circle framing the star.

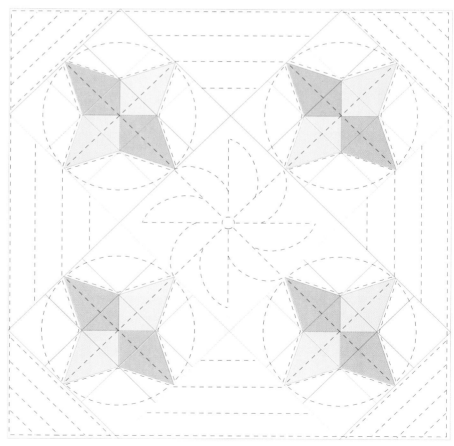

FIG 70

◄ FIG 70A A symmetrical repeating curve can be used in the sashing to make a scalloped frame for the basket block...

► FIG 70B ... and a larger curve across the sashing strips puts a circular frame around each of the baskets.

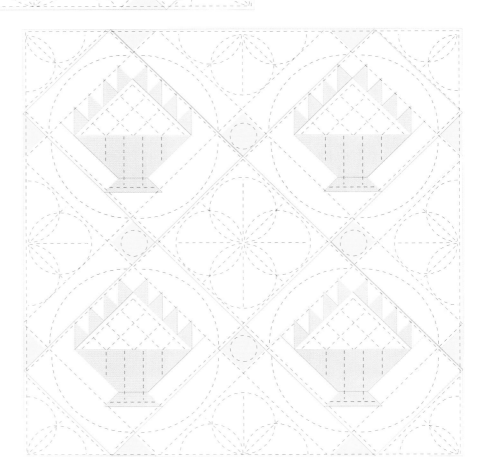

▲ FIG 70C Your quilting choices for plain blocks or other areas of the quilt will influence
what you put in the other areas – here the circle of the feather wreath is reflected in the
circle around the basket blocks, but the overall balance is a little uneven...

⬛ FIG 70D   ... whereas doubling or repeating the larger simple curve looks more satisfactory.

SQUARE MEDALLION SETTING

Like the main and plain setting, this medallion style is another wonderful way of making a little do a lot and looks good whether you have used pieced or appliqué blocks. It is particularly favoured by those who love quilting (hand or machine) and who want to leave "lots of space for quilting" and the assumption is that because this setting delivers the maximum quilting space short of wholecloth, the texture should be complex and demanding of attention in its own right. Again, unless you have a very clear idea of what you will quilt in these large spaces from the outset, it can be quite intimidating to confront them once the top is put together.

If the main quilt blocks are large and complex, it might be worth considering using a simple background pattern in the open spaces to give a basic texture that will high-light the detail rather than competing with it. On the other hand, if the main blocks are large and uncomplicated, you will probably want to have medium to high-density texture across the whole quilt to enhance and lift the overall effect. For simple main blocks you will want to look at quilting possibilities within the main shapes in addition to the outline quilting in order to avoid having large areas devoid

FIG 71

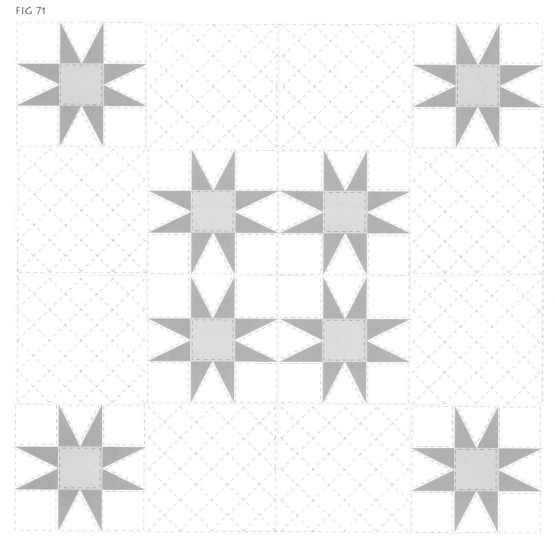

FIG 71A Large spaces and straight-set blocks may seem to call for quantities of com-plex quilting. As you review some of the possibilities, which could of course include commercial pat-terns, look first at one or two very basic options, per-haps beginning with a regular crosshatch or grid.

of texture (heaven forbid!). By judicious use of the halving principle and simple quilting, it is possible to make even the largest and most basic block appear more complex than it really is.

The blocks might have a strongly graphic and interesting outline, which could be repeated or adapted in the alternating empty spaces for a positive/negative effect. Review some of the possibilities for adapting an appliqué or embroidery pattern to fit the space and whilst you are in a reflective mood, turn your thoughts to incorporating cording and stuffing or trapunto techniques into the "regular" quilting – the extra definition of trapunto may add that extra sparkle to the finished piece.

Remember that there are cues and clues for you in the shapes used in the blocks, fabric styles, colours and patterns. Whilst there are always exceptions to the rule (and it is worth repeating here that in quilting there are no rules), this particular quilt setting can have a very traditional appearance – perhaps this could be a cue to look for traditional style patterns and motifs to adapt to fit the spaces. Ornate feather swags, loops and swirls, or multi-strand cables might be suitable choices – check out the wonderful variety of stencils available for these types of patterns.

FIG 71B Using curved lines instead of straight to divide up the empty border spaces could be the start of something completely different – what if you went on from here to fill in these new spaces with different textures or more curved lines?

FIG 72

FIG 72   Curved-line divisions of space could serve as a frame for a simple motif which could be reflected or repeated in the centre space. Have some fun adding lines of your own to this quilt plan!

FIG 73

◄ FIG 73A   A number of possibil-ities are shown in this medallion setting of an Oak Leaf block – dividing up the empty space with connecting straight lines to use as a design grid, using straight line texture alone, repeating the appliqué motif or elements taken from it as a quilting design, adding a simple large-scale motif, or a formal feather swag. None of these illustrations provides the perfect solution, but there may be ideas you could develop to suit yourself.

◄ FIG 73B   The by-now-familiar crosshatch or grid gives a good contrast to the curves of the appliqué blocks and would be a pleasing texture, but could you do more interesting things with all that space?

◄ FIG 73C Straight parallel lines that change direction at the mid-point of each side might look more interesting than the grid option.

► FIG 73D Using shorter straight lines to form a basketweave style of texture is easy to do and gives a more complex surface.

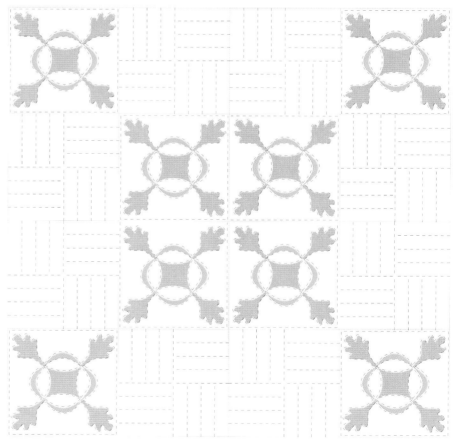

◀ FIG 73E   Sometimes, just repeating the main lines of the block works well as the basis for deciding how to fill space.

▶ FIG 73F   Take care to keep a good proportion and balance between the scale of the main block and that of the quilting motif – here you would probably want to add further lines to the motif or perhaps fractionally reduce its size.

▲FIG 73G The close meander quilting suggested here at the centre will give a rich texture to that area as well as highlighting the four central blocks and contrast with the
"ribbing" effect of the straight parallel lines that extend into the border area.
Extending background quilting into a border can produce new and interesting shapes.
The feathered swags indicated here add complexity but would need to be more flowing
and tailored to fit the space to maximum effect.

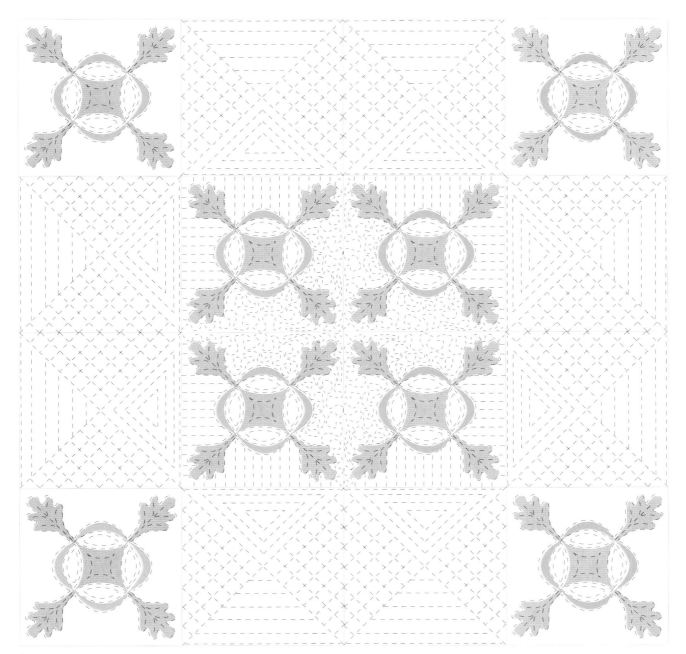

FIG 73H A mixture of straight-line patterns that are easy to mark and stitch contrast with the meander quilting at the centre and maintain a reasonably even spread of texture, but beware the perils of using too many different ideas in one piece.

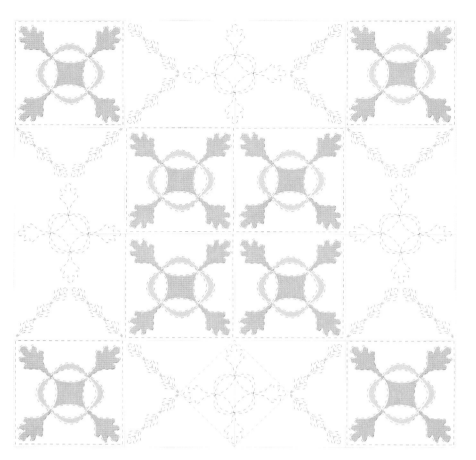

◄ FIG 73I   Variations on a theme – using repeats of the main block as quilting patterns and extending them with an element from the block (in this case a leaf). Without additional quilting in the form of background texture, the scale of this solution is not a satisfactory balance between quilted and unquilted space.

► FIG 73J   A marginally improved balance of quilted/unquilted space makes the overall look at this stage quite appealing.

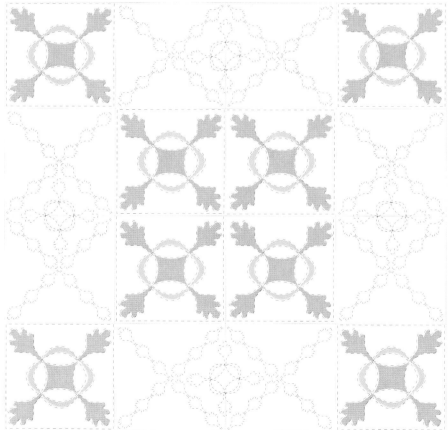

FIG 74

FIG 74A On the following pages you can see that different textures within a simple curved-line framework will each have their own particular effect. No claims are made for the perfection or "rightness" of any of the suggestions, but they may spark off some ideas of your own. In the quilt illustrated above, the spider-web curves work well up to a point – complete rather than partial "webs" would probably have a more finished look.

FIG 74B Taking the framing curves from the illustration on the opposite page, echoing them once, and then filling the background spaces with straight lines puts a little stronger emphasis on all the appliqué blocks.

▲FIG 74C   Filling the same curved frame with diagonal parallel lines gives emphasis to the main blocks but is not completely satisfactory.

▲FIG 74D   This almost works – perhaps it could be improved by omitting the half circles framing the four corner blocks and running the rippling curves right up to the edges of each appliqué block. On the other hand, remember that you do not have to like every single possibility that you come up with when developing quilting plans!

FIG 75

▲ FIG 75   A medallion setting of three pieced blocks and no empty spaces to fill!
A framework of straight lines is shown – where would you go from here?

SAMPLER QUILTS

Making this type of quilt is probably the best and most popular way of learning a variety of techniques for both piecing and appliqué. When it comes to the quilting, however, it can be difficult to know what to do and where to start, because all the blocks are so different! Some of your quilting options will depend on the selection of blocks you have used in your sampler.

Many samplers are made using what is known as the quilt-as-you go technique, where each block is finished, layered, basted and quilted before the final joining together into a quilt. This means that some, if not all, of the quilting decisions for the blocks have already been made along the way, so in this instance you may be focusing more on how to quilt the sashings and borders and thinking about using flowing linear patterns rather than separate motifs as a good way of linking and connecting the blocks.

If you have not used the quilt-as-you-go construction method, you have no such restrictions. You could treat the whole quilt top as one large piece rather than an arrangement of individual blocks and work an overall quilting pattern across the entire area e.g. baptist fan, grid, clamshell. This may sound outrageous, but can be surprising effective in terms of looking good and blending together the different blocks. If you have to consider sashing strips as part of your quilt, you could choose one overall pattern to work across the blocks (say, clamshell) and linear patterns for the sashings and border. Or you could use a different overall pattern for each block so that the finished quilt is a sampler of quilted texture as well as piecing and appliqué techniques. Another possibility would be to use the same style of background quilting for each block, for instance, all straight lines or all curved-line patterns.

This award-winning quilt by Susie Corke is an admirable example of using simple quilting ideas to great effect – of course it also helps that Susie's hand quilting is exquisite! Outline and echo quilting combine with a simple motif repeated in each of the sampler blocks.

FIG 76

Look for any similarities in the blocks. Perhaps a number of them have a particular orientation, say diagonal rather than vertical, which you could emphasise by the direction of the quilting lines within each block.

Bear in mind that sampler quilts are delightfully varied by their very nature and there is plenty to attract the viewer's attention – the two most important factors to consider for quilting are to keep it simple and to have an even density of quilting.

◄▲ FIG 76A+B   Sampler quilts have a particular charm – a variety of blocks, colours and shapes.
Illustrated here are some suggestions for introducing some continuity with quilting choices
for sashings and borders (see also section on Sashings and Borders). Take a few moments to
consider how you would go about planning the quilting for the blocks themselves – are there
any elements from the blocks that could be adapted? What textures could be introduced?

▲ FIG 76C   Even before you think about how to quilt the individual sampler blocks, you can have fun using the halving principle and straight lines to construct simple patterns for the sashings and borders.

▲ FIG 76D   Still simple, still straight lines and just as easy to mark and quilt as the suggestion on the facing page!

LOG CABIN QUILTS

The Log Cabin quilt is a perennial favourite and one which has endless scope in its variations and settings. The "how do I quilt it?" question in this case will be guided by the factors of time available and preferred technique as well as any cues and clues from the quilt itself.

Practicalities

If the blocks have been worked on non-paper foundations, there will be an additional layer to consider, in which case you may decide that it would be easier to quilt by machine than by hand.

A considerable proportion of a Log Cabin quilt will have underlying seam allowances because of the way it is made and they will be even more pronounced if the strips themselves are narrow. Again this will affect the ease of hand quilting and you might want to consider quilting within rather than along the seam lines to avoid the allowances.

Outline quilting each seam of each block will produce an even spread of texture, but could be soul-destroying to stitch because it is time-consuming and boring. It can also be unsatisfactory because it produces no obvious additional texture.

Cues and clues

The strongly graphic nature of this type of quilt lends itself to strong simple quilting treatments that follow and emphasise the main design lines.

It is possible that a variety of fabrics have been used as Log Cabin is suited to scraps. This is another reason for keeping things simple, particularly if the majority of the fabrics are prints – remember that complex quilting patterns do not show as well on prints as they do on plains.

Smooth curving lines can work well because they can give a feeling of movement and contrast with the many straight lines of the Log Cabin piecing.

Log Cabin quilts made by Jenny Otto (top left), Rosalind Leslie (top right) and Mandy Fanthom (front centre). Mandy's quilt is based on one of the variations shown on pages163.

FIG 77

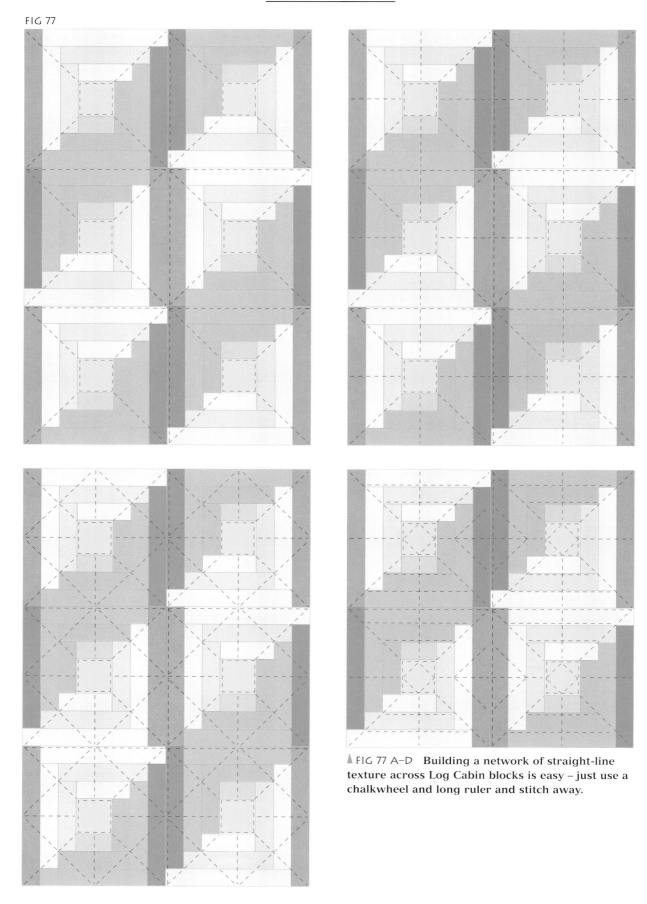

▲ FIG 77 A–D   Building a network of straight-line texture across Log Cabin blocks is easy – just use a chalkwheel and long ruler and stitch away.

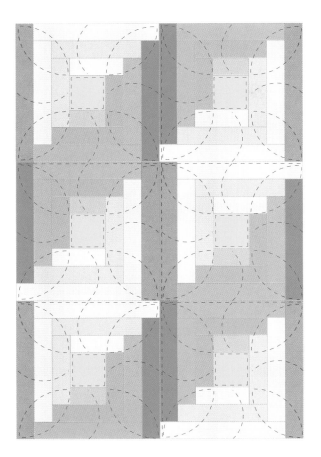

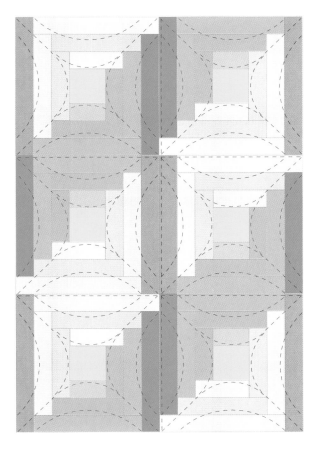

▲ FIG 77 E–G   Curved lines are just as much fun and possibly even more effective than straight lines – certainly they contrast well with the strong diagonals of the pattern and its numerous straight seam lines.

FIG 78

▲ FIG 78 **An even spread of straight-line texture with some changes of line direction for added interest.**

STRIP-PIECED QUILTS

Like Log Cabin there are plenty of seam allowances to consider in this type of quilt, in addition to which the strips may be of equal or varying width. Again, there may be very little space to quilt within the strips, so working across and ignoring the seam lines, or stitching between them, may make things easier.

Some traditional strip-pieced quilt blocks and settings such as Rail Fence or Roman Stripe have a well-defined overall structure that can be used as a design grid to plan the quilting. You could start, using the halving principle, from the seams that join the blocks together, remembering that curved lines, or a mixture of curved and straight lines, could work well and contrast with the straight lines of the strips, or you could choose to work within each individual block, depending on what you think looks best. More contemporary quilt formats and abstract block arrangements along the lines of Margaret Miller's "Strips that sizzle" may be suitable for a less rigidly based quilting plan. Think perhaps of dividing the quilt top into irregularly sized areas of differing textures or drawing an assortment of freehand lines across the whole quilt.

Outline quilting of the strips in the main triangles and some easy quilting options for the background space.

This small Rail Fence quilt illustrates one of the perils of quilting on "busy" prints – the diagonal parallel lines quilted across the blocks hardly show, whereas the cable pattern in the plain border is very clear.

129

FIG 79

◄▲FIG 79   Four very basic quilting solutions –
depending on the size of the blocks and width of
strips, further quilting could be added.

FIG 80

◄▲ FIG 80 Outline quilting and easy straight-line divisions of the "blank" triangle are almost as effective as the half-motif made up of shallow curves.

FIG 81

⬛ FIG 81 A – B   The simple braid pattern here is built up from equal-width strips that call for uncomplicated linear patterns, curved or straight.

▲ FIG 81 C–D   Large curves, shorter curves – both these quilting solutions are easy to draft because they are based on the seam lines within the braid strips.

▲ FIG 81 E–F   Straight lines or curves, again based on the skeleton of the pieced braid – you may find that the contrast of the curves is more pleasing.

▲ FIG 81 G – H   Two very basic quilting plans, both of which could be considerably expanded by additional lines.

FIG 82

▲▶ FIG 82 Altering what is quilted on just one of the three sides of the Tumbling
Block pattern can make a subtle difference. It will, of course, depend on the size
and scale of the diamonds as to how much space is available for quilting.

ONE-SHAPE QUILTS

This is piecing at its simplest – to take one shape and repeat it and repeat it until you have enough for a quilt. There are many beautiful examples of this type of quilt in historical collections where hexagons, diamonds or squares have been organised into complex and intricate patterns.

More recently, there has been a tremendous interest in the colourwash techniques so superbly pioneered by Deirdre Amsden where many squares (or other simple tessellating shapes) of different print fabrics are graded and arranged into an abstract format.

One-shape quilts may have been worked over papers (otherwise known as English piecing), or they may have been put together using the speedy "stitch and slice" technique, or by basic hand or machine piecing. Whichever technique has been used for this type of quilt, you will have a great number of seam allowances to consider. Also, depending on the actual size of the shape used, there may be very little space to quilt inside the seams. One simple quilting option might be just to outline the major shapes and/or areas rather than outlining every single piece which, as in the case of many Log Cabin quilts, could be very tedious to do and produce little visual impact.

Tying can be most effective and has a strong and ample historical precedent. Such quilts usually have a backing only, dispensing with batting to make a coverlet rather than a quilt in the true sense of the word.

FIG 83

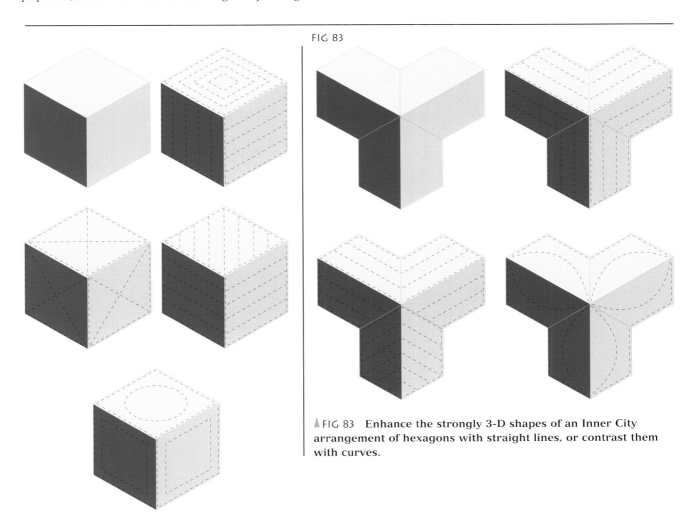

▲ FIG 83 Enhance the strongly 3-D shapes of an Inner City arrangement of hexagons with straight lines, or contrast them with curves.

FIG 84

▲ FIG 84 Simplicity and even texture are major considerations, although there may be scope to leave some areas free of quilting.

FIG 85

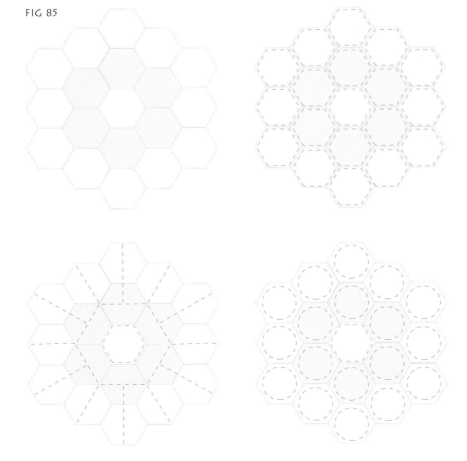

The strong curves and swirls of the freehand quilting in the background contrast beautifully with the strong tessellating 3D shapes of the Inner City blocks. Hand pieced and quilted by Elaine Hammond.

◄► FIG 85 Quilting circles inside each hexagon may be easier than outline quilting, or you could try halving the hexagons with straight or curved lines in a variety of ways as shown here and overleaf. Which would be faster to quilt?

139

FIG 85 (CONT.)

AMISH-STYLE QUILTS

Amongst the most recognised and covetable examples of this widely admired quilting tradition, Diamond in Square and Bars (this page and overleaf) are straightforward to piece and have positively acres of space for quilting.

You may be more inclined to choose hand quilting as your preferred technique for this style of quilt, although competent machine quilters will enjoy the challenge presented by some of the Amish quilting patterns. Whichever stitching technique you select, there are many excellent books and patterns available to help you follow the traditional Amish format.

For something that little bit different you could have fun developing some ideas of your own working with the halving principle to divide up the large spaces. If you have chosen plain fabrics, any quilting you do is going to show sufficiently clearly to justify using quite complex quilting patterns - remember to give some thought to the scale of the patterns so they fit the spaces well and give an appearance of even texture.

Contrasting types of texture such as close gridding or crosshatching set against curving cable or feather patterns are often particularly effective in this type of quilt. In fact, many of the simple background quilting patterns like clamshell or wineglass can look stunning in this context and should never be dismissed on the grounds of being too mundane or ordinary.

Strong colours and a traditional Amish-style format are the basis for this wonderful quilt made by Martha Preston and Vivienne Coles. If you look closely at the quilting designs, you can appreciate the balance and simplicity underlying the richly textured effect.

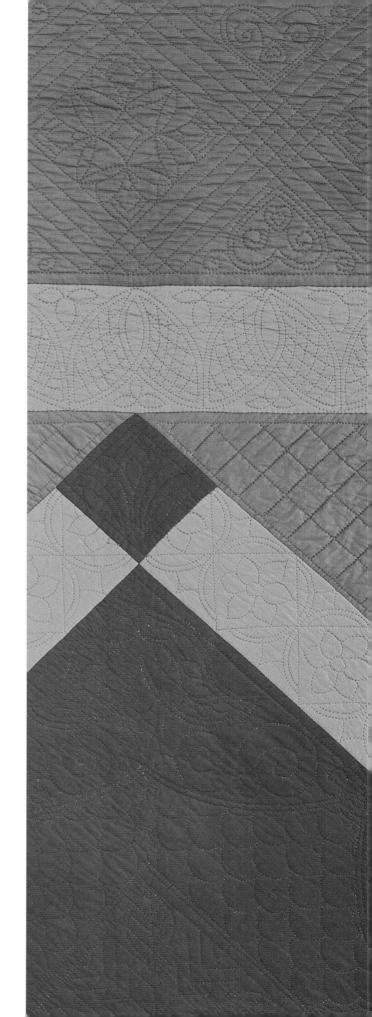

FIG 86

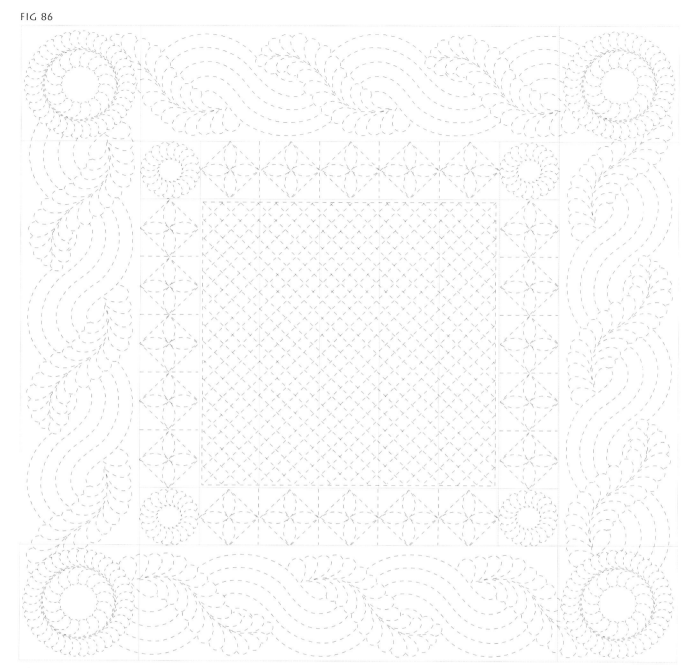

⊿FIG 86 Large open areas, strong geometric shapes and intricate quilting are hallmarks of the best of the Amish tradition – here you can see how contrasting texture works to achieve a harmonious whole. The central bars or strips have the simplest of textures in the straight lines of the crosshatch or grid, straight lines and curves in the "pumpkin seed" inner border, and glorious sweeping curves of the feather/cable outer border.

FIG 87

▲ FIG 87   Here there is good contrast between the crosshatched areas and the open lines of the roses and fiddlehead ferns.

SASHINGS AND BORDERS

Sashings and borders are often much neglected in quilting terms simply because they are viewed as difficult or awkward. For these areas the question of "how do I quilt it?" is often resolved by looking for printed patterns and stencils that are the right width and style – a quest that can be lengthy and not always one hundred per cent successful. If you have not already chosen a pattern or patterns for the sashings and border by the time the quilt top is completed, you might like to try using the halving principle to develop some ideas of your own. The advantage of using this principle is that the pattern will fit the space and be of a scale that looks "right" in terms of proportion to the quilt as a whole.

Use the main blocks of the quilt to provide an initial design grid so that you have a starting point for halving the spaces. You can then go further and look at the possibilities of using some or all of the seam lines within the block to divide these spaces further. Remember, there is no need to include all the dividing lines in the final pattern. Some or all of them can be omitted after they have served as a guide. If you know that you want to use repeats of a particular motif to make a sashing or border pattern, halving and dividing up spaces in this way will serve as a good general guide to the appropriate scale and placement for the motif you have chosen.

If the quilt has more than one border, it may be preferable to have the quilting patterns for each border related to each other to give a feeling of continuity and cohesion. This relationship can be achieved by using one motif as the basis for a pattern and changing the scale and number of repeats from one border to another.

CUES AND CLUES

As we have seen in the case of single blocks and full quilts, you do not have to pluck quilting ideas from thin air when wondering how to quilt sashings and borders. In addition to the halving

principle, there may be cues and clues from the blocks and fabrics used in the main part of the quilt top which are there offering suggestions.

One possibility might be to repeat the block, or the main elements from it, to create a border quilting pattern – squares, triangles and circles all have great potential here, as do the leaves and flowers featured in many traditional appliqué designs. You could also think about distorting the block, or just one section of it, and drafting it as a rectangle based on the border depth. This can be done with graph or squared paper, ruler and pencil, and computer-friendly quilters will enjoy exploring their favourite quilting and drawing programmes for this particular feature.

Consider taking a background quilting treatment and using it for the sashings and borders. If the sashing and/or border fabrics are heavily patterned, this may be a good way of achieving that all-important even spread of texture without any loss of pattern definition. Clamshell, grid or crosshatch, paired parallel lines, diamonds and wineglass are all simple but very effective background patterns in this respect. Look at back-ground patterns to see if they "contain" or suggest another pattern; for example, grid or crosshatch contains a pattern of single squares point to point.

Look also at the dominant fabric(s) in the quilt top for any motifs that could be adapted and arranged into a linear quilting pattern by adding one or more simple linking lines – for instance, a basic leaf shape could be repeated and linked together with a short curved line.

Border upon border – different textures, different ideas, nothing complex. Quilts by Susie Corke, Mary Christie, Joan Loudon.

Detail of "Topsy" by Sandie Lush. Notice the spacing of the line echoing the main shape of the pieced block and the use of crosshatching to blend the background texture across the sashing strips.

PRACTICALITIES

Perhaps the first practical requirement in the actual quilting of sashings and borders is to quilt as close as possible against each sashing and border seam. This is not visually interesting or productive quilting, nor does it necessarily call for precise marking beforehand, but whichever side of the seams it is done on, it will give a crisper overall definition to the final texture of the quilt.

If you plan to hand quilt, you will want to avoid too much stitching through seam allowances, so you might choose patterns for the sashings and borders that fit comfortably into the seam-free space. This may leave a slight rise in the fabric on either side of the quilting, in which case you can add an extra straight line of stitching close to the seam lines as a way of reducing this fullness.

Bear in mind how much the final texture of your planned pattern will show if either sashings or borders are printed rather than plain fabrics.

The general rule of keeping it simple on patterned fabrics applies equally to both sashings and borders, as does maintaining an overall balance of texture density.

A flexicurve, ruler and chalk wheel are all excellent tools you can use to try out various ideas on the quilt top without making any firm commitment to a final decision.

A border is a vital part of the final "statement" of any quilt and should frame and complement the main design of the quilt. A border may even contrast with the main design of the quilt to produce this desired result. Whatever the pattern choices for any border, the spread of texture should appear to be even and the pattern should fit comfortably within the border space – nothing looks worse than a pattern that is too skimpy for the space in which it is set.

One of the background quilting patterns from the main quilt can be run over and across the seam lines to meet the main border pattern, and a different fill-in or background quilting can then run from the outer edge of border pattern right up to the binding. This will add more visual interest to the overall texture for very little extra effort.

Very narrow sashings may look better if the quilting is restricted to lines running parallel and close to the seams. Patterns of a suitably small scale to fit the space may be hard to find. However, sashings wider than one inch almost always look better if they have some planned quilting treatment or pattern assigned to them rather than just these parallel lines.

Whether you are quilting by hand or machine, you might want to consider the advantages of stitching from the centre outwards to the edge of sashings and borders rather than beginning at one edge and working along to the next side. Remember that all quilting pushes the fabric fractionally ahead of the needle so that there is some movement. If your chosen pattern involves a number of changes in stitching direction, there will be less distortion along the length of the border or sashing if you work outwards from the halfway point.

If, despite your best efforts during the quilt construction process, you find yourself looking at borders that have an endearingly rippled outer edge, all is not lost. It is possible to contain and reduce this rippling by working evenly spaced lines of quilting across the width of all four border strips. In this case your quilting plan could incorporate a number of horizontal lines or even be structured on horizontal rather than longitudinal lines – in other words, have the pattern run across the borders rather than along them.

FIG 88

▲ FIG 88   With some of the decisions made at the centre of the quilt the borders can be divided up into sections as a starting point for drafting your own patterns or arranging motifs

FIG 89

FIG 90

FIG 91

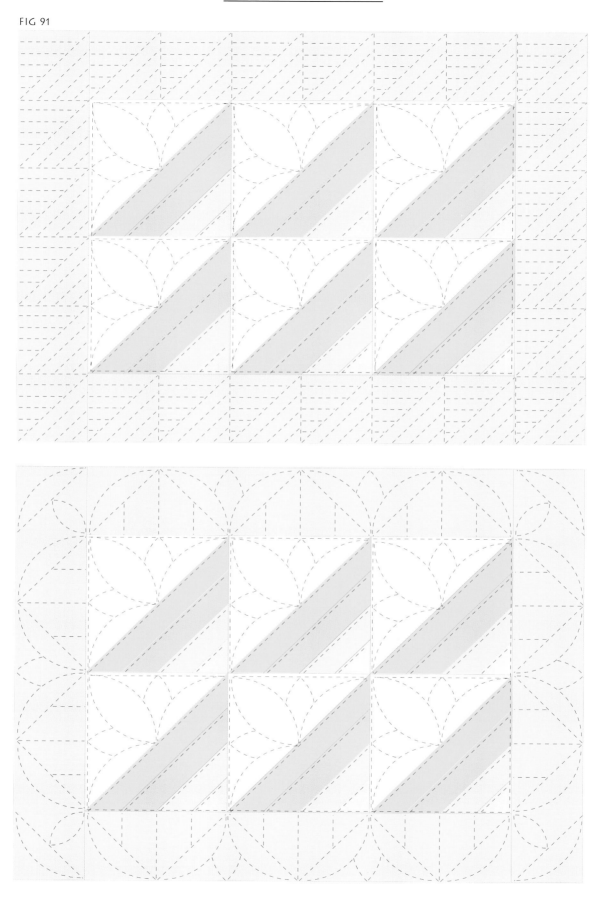

FIG 92

FIG 93

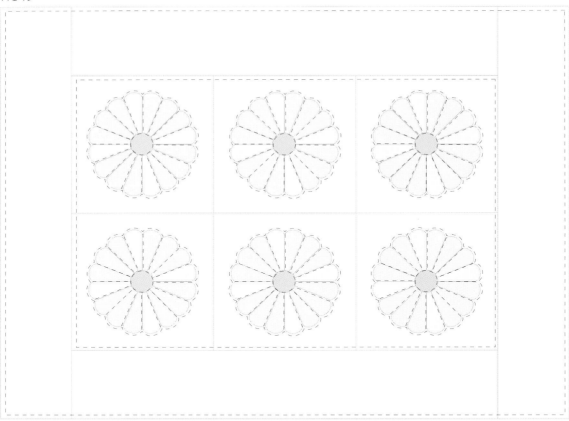

▲ FIG 93A   Outline quilting against the inner and outer edges of the border will help with the overall definition. A variety of easy-to-draft options for both borders and backgrounds is explored over the following pages – look at them carefully to form your own opinion of what works well and what does not. Notice the various straight-line options for quilting between the main blocks. Think about how you could develop the simpler borders – for instance, motifs could be added within some of the spaces or main lines echoed.

FIG 89 (PAGE 150-1)   Use the skeleton or seam lines of the blocks to suggest starting points for your own border designs.

FIG 90 (PAGE 151)   In this instance, using some of the block seam lines as a basis for planning the border quilting got a little out of hand! The initial division lines (shown in red) gave an interesting saw-tooth pattern, but filling this in with parallel lines made it look overly fussy.

FIG 91 (PAGE 152)   Both borders would be equally easy to mark and quilt – you may find one more appealing than the other.

FIG 92 (PAGE 153)   Two more simple border solutions which are originally based on main block seams and both of which could be developed a little further.

FIG 93B   A very basic border using straight lines – more lines or motifs could be added.

FIG 93 C – D (PAGE 156)   Diagonal straight lines which change direction – notice the two different options for the space between the blocks.

FIG 93E (PAGE 157 TOP)   This placement of straight lines gives an even spread of texture, but looks rather rigid and uninteresting.

FIG 93F (PAGE 157 BOTTOM)   Short curves make a cable effect along the major seam lines and outer edge of the border – this could be improved by changing the texture in the border.

FIG 93G (PAGE 158 TOP)   Extending the background quilting into the border and using a half Dresden Plate for the outer border.

FIG 93H (PAGE 158 BOTTOM)   Using main seam lines and halving with curved lines produces a pleasing border outline which could be developed further.

FIG 93I (PAGE 159 TOP)   Variation on a curved line still using main seam lines as the starting point.

FIG 93J (PAGE 159 BOTTOM)   Repeating half of the Dresden Plate as a quilting pattern and using the main seam lines as a base to fill in with easy curves.

FIG 94A (PAGE 160 TOP)   The straight lines of crosshatching or gridding add texture to the border space and effectively contrast with the curves of the main pattern.

FIG 94B (PAGE 160 BOTTOM)   An effective border of overlapping circles using the block seam lines as a division guide would be easy to stitch – an added bonus is the motif which is created at the corners.

FIG 94C (PAGE 161 TOP)   This curved-line variation uses shallow curves within divisions of the border based on the block seam lines.

FIG 94D (PAGE 161 BOTTOM)   More shallow curves and yet another possibility – would you add any further lines to this border pattern?

FIG 93 (CONT.)

FIG 93 (CONT.)

FIG 94

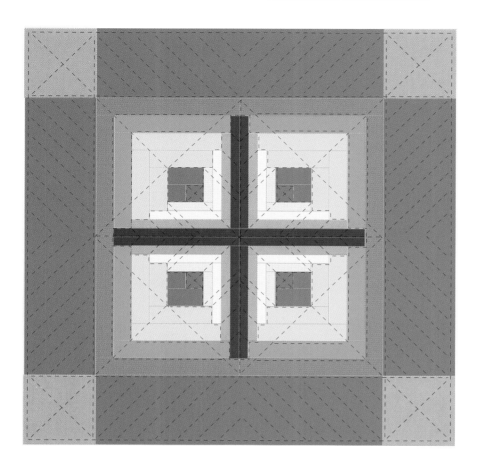

FIG 95 Four straight-line possibilities for a Log Cabin quilt – plain background-type texture or patterns based on the halving principle. Overleaf, a simple curved-line border pattern frames four different curved line possibilities for the border of a Log Cabin quilt, ranging from the simplicity of crosshatching or gridding and parallel diagonal lines switching direction, to slightly more complex straight-line patterns based on the halving principle.

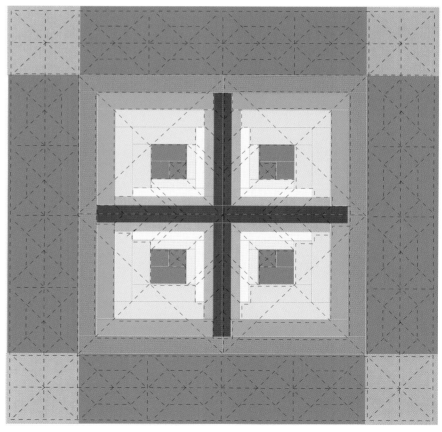

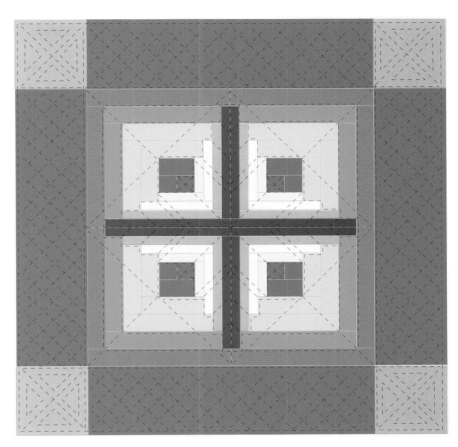

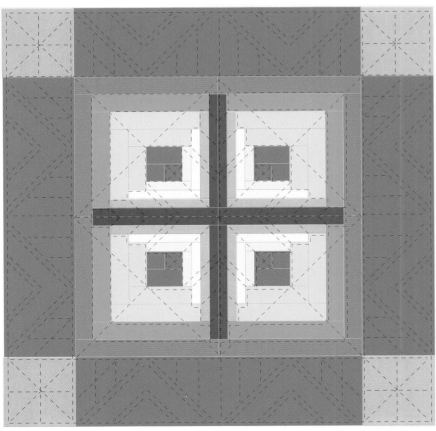

FIG 95 (CONT.)

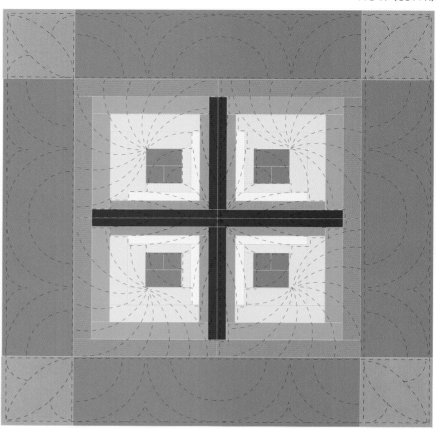

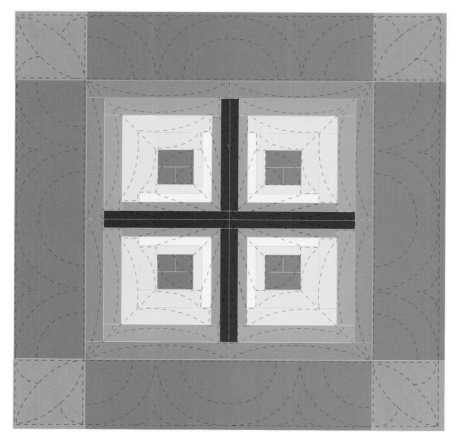

◄▲► FIG 95 Here the same curved line border is repeated on all four quilts – think about what additions you could make to these basic lines to fill in some of the space. Would you use straight lines or more curves? Notice that the curved line patterns across the four main blocks are different – does one enhance and contrast with the straight lines of the piecing better than the others? Does one seem to fit better with the border pattern?

(Clue: there are no right answers to these questions!)

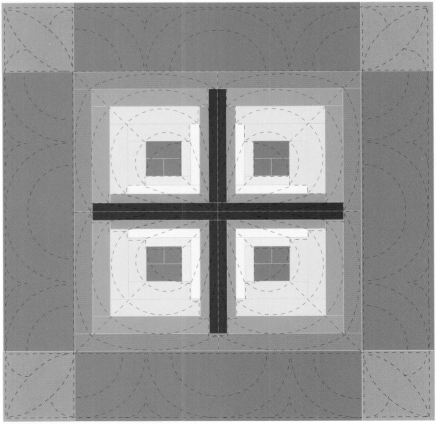

FIG 96

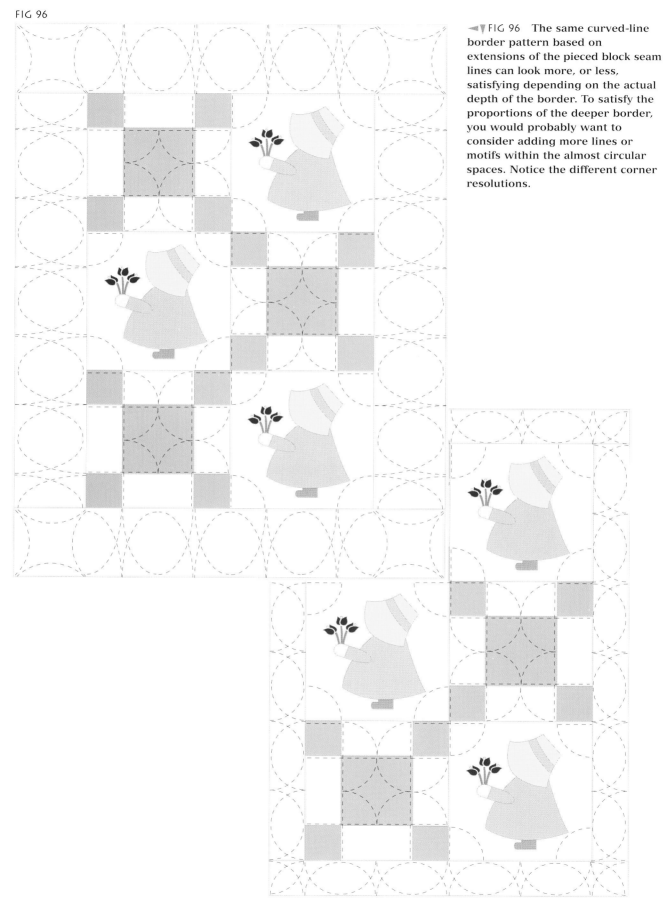

FIG 96   The same curved-line border pattern based on extensions of the pieced block seam lines can look more, or less, satisfying depending on the actual depth of the border. To satisfy the proportions of the deeper border, you would probably want to consider adding more lines or motifs within the almost circular spaces. Notice the different corner resolutions.

FIG 97

◀▼FIG 97 Taking cues and clues for quilting patterns from the flowers and leaves in one of the quilt blocks. And, of course, there is always more than one easy way to arrange the flowers and leaves within the border space! The dashed red lines show how the border was divided up to give a guide for the placing of the motifs.

FIG 98

◀▼FIG 98 The border of this appliqué quilt has been divided up and a curved line flipped and repeated. Flowers and leaves arranged along the curved line are quilted repeats of those in the appliqué blocks. Notice that the only difference between these two quilts is at the corners – one has a narrow open loop, the other a rounder closed loop – and see how tiny the differences are when these loops have leaves arranged along them. An object lesson in not trying to be too clever! A better alternative option would have been to run the flower and leaf pattern diagonally across the corners and fill in the remaining triangle with a flower shape.

FIG 99

◀▼FIG 99 A–B Two of the possible starting points for developing quilting solutions for the sashing strips – you may find the frame formed by the longer curves more appealing, but both suggestions are capable of being developed further into more interesting linear patterns.

▲ FIG 99C Steps one and two in dividing up the space in both sashing and border and beginning to develop a simple border pattern. The use of curved lines around the main appliqué blocks gives a pleasing framed effect, although it would be very easy to add more lines to this pattern so that it filled the width of the sashing more completely to make a more formal grid type of frame for the blocks. From the first single line of the repeating curve in the border, it is a short step to adding an extra curve for a rippling ribbon effect. Pause here and consider the options for filling in the remaining spaces with different textures.

▲ FIG 99D   The third and fourth steps in completing a linked cable pattern for the border. The outer curved lines framing the blocks could be similarly emphasised by this doubling procedure, which might be rather interesting. Notice how much scope remains for adding motifs within the border pattern and in the large outer triangles, and remember that there are plenty of cues and clues to help you – look at the centre shape of the appliqué blocks for instance, or the leaf shapes. All of the main appliqué and quilting pattern elements so far are curved – consider introducing some straight-line texture for heightened contrast.

▲ FIG 99E   Straight-line texture, in the form of parallel lines switching direction, has been added to the background, whilst maintaining the original curved frame to the appliqué blocks. Does this work well, or would it have looked better with a simpler, less directional texture? A different border pattern has been used – is this an improvement on the linked cable, or is it just different? Now all you have to think about is what to do with the background space in the appliqué blocks…

FIG 100

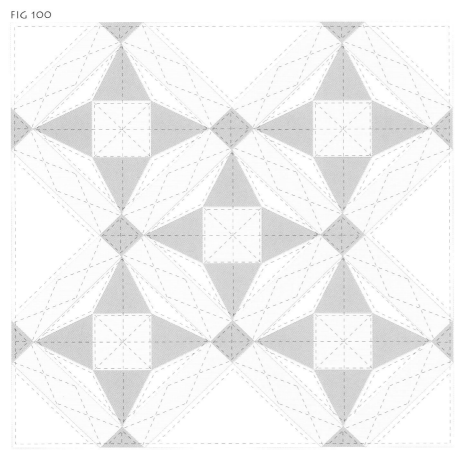

FIG 100 Straight lines can look just as effective as shallow curving lines; both lead the eye easily along the length of the sashing strips. The empty triangular spaces could be filled with either straight-line or curved texture, eg crosshatch/grid or clamshell, or you could consider echoing the triangle with straight lines. Think about some of the ways you could divide and fill these spaces.

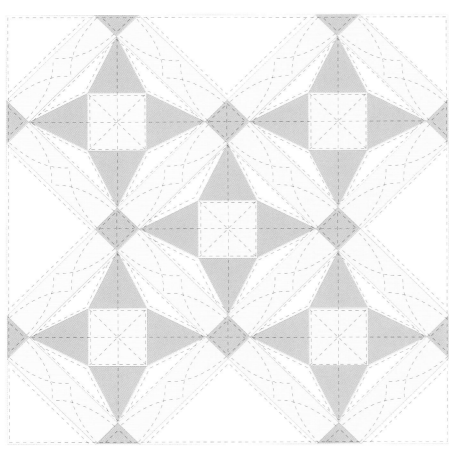

FIG 101

◄ FIG 101A   Notice how the choice of quilting pattern for the sashing can change the perception of framing and highlighting the main blocks. The trefoil motif used in the triangular spaces is based on the shapes of the appliqué blocks.

▼ FIG 101B   Dividing up the triangular spaces by echoing a scalloped line puts a different emphasis on the main blocks – the curve of the scallops could face either out from the centre as shown here, or in towards the centre as indicated in the corner triangles.

▲ FIG 101C   Not quite echo quilting in the outer triangles, but straight parallel lines which change direction and reflect the on-point setting of the blocks – easy to mark and quilt and a good contrast with the curved shapes of the appliqué. Consider the effect of using a similar straight-line texture in the background areas of the blocks.

PATTERNS

On the following pages you will find a collection of quilting ideas that have been based on easy divisions of a square and predominantly curved lines. As you browse through them, I hope you will see just how easy it is to play with the halving principle and some simple curves. Red marks show main divisions and halfway points to help you analyse how some patterns were developed. If you are anxious to practise your hand or machine quilting skills, any one of these patterns would be a great starting point. Maybe there is an empty square in a pieced block or even a completely empty block in a quilt just waiting to be quilted? Perhaps one of them could be repeated to form a border or sashing design? By now you will have realised that the possibilities for creating your own quilting solutions are limited only by your imagination, but begin very humbly. Turn the pages and enjoy!

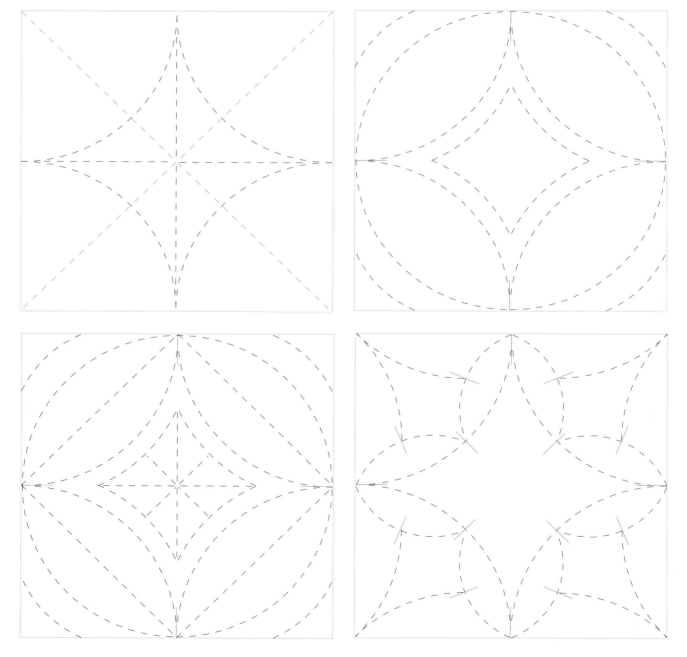

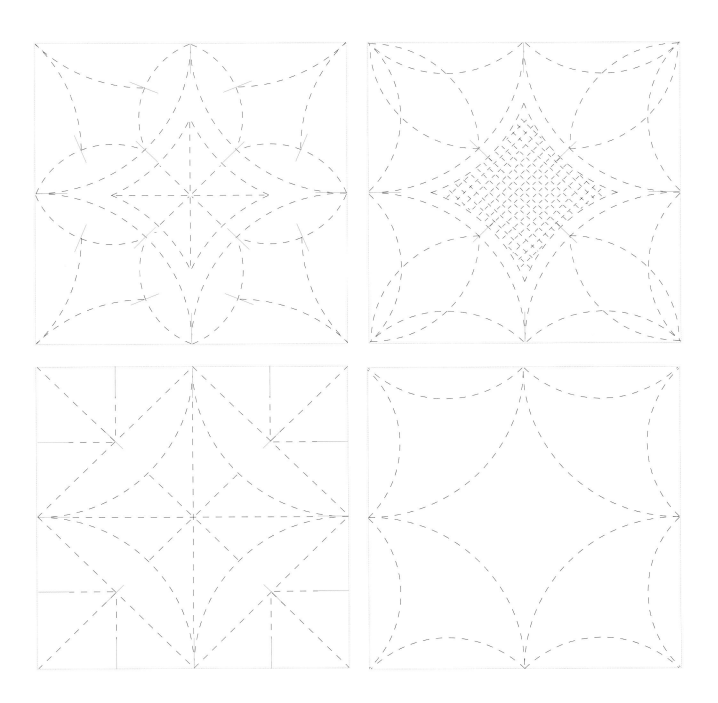

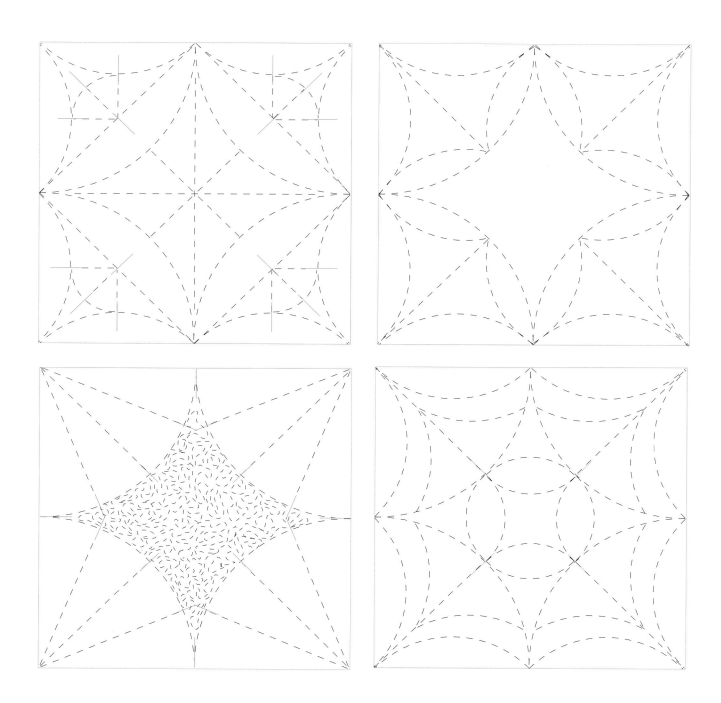

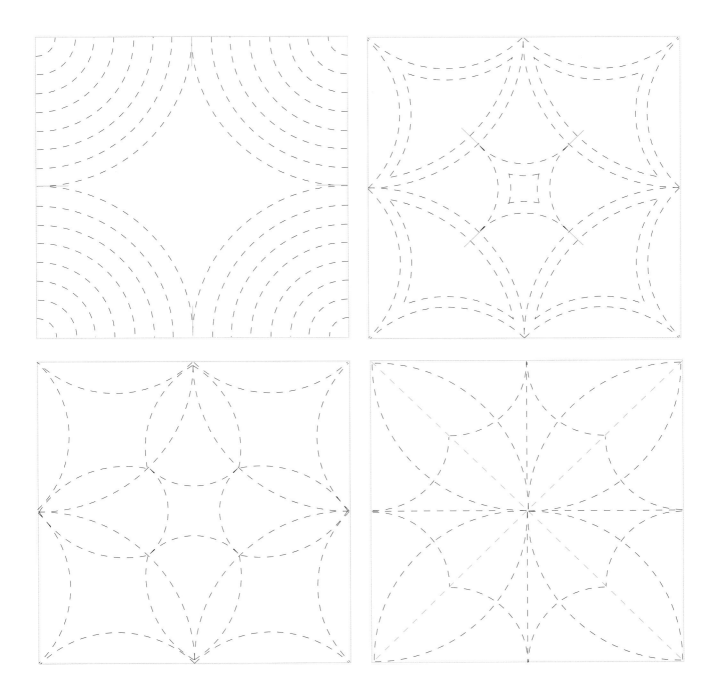

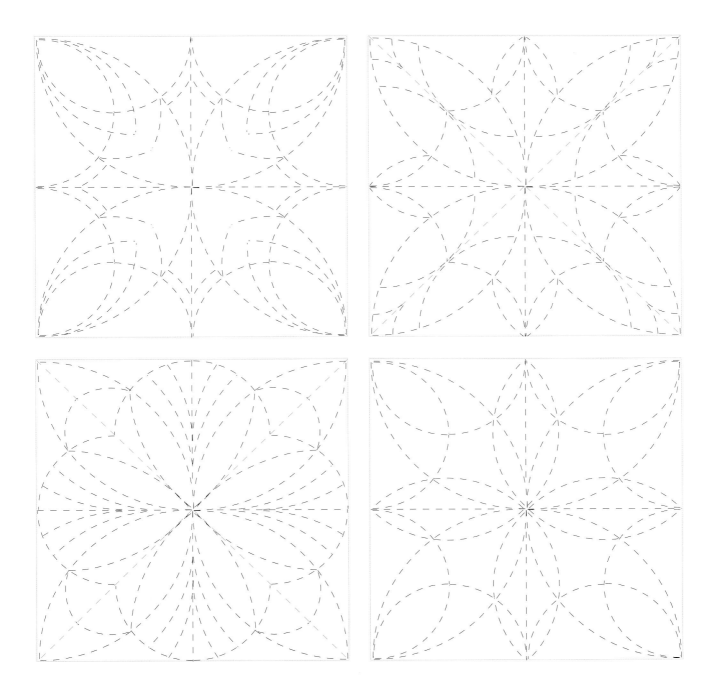

181

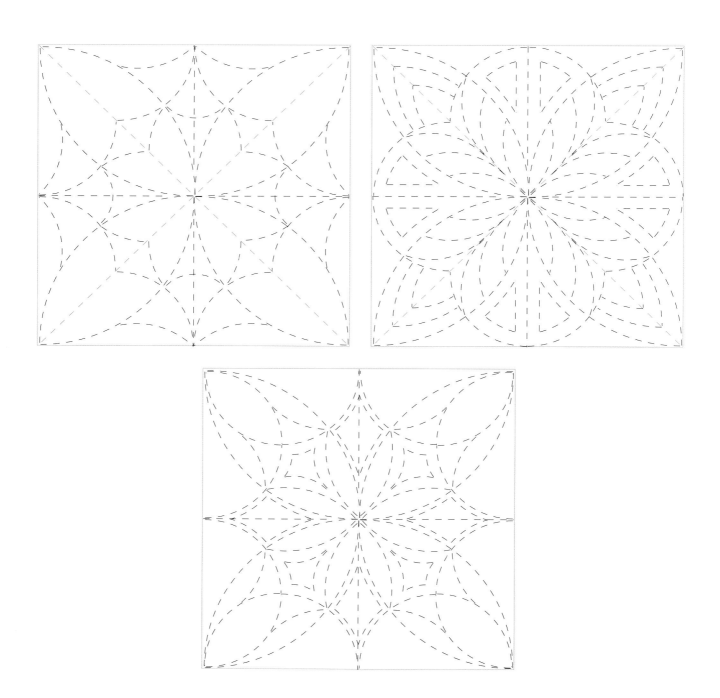

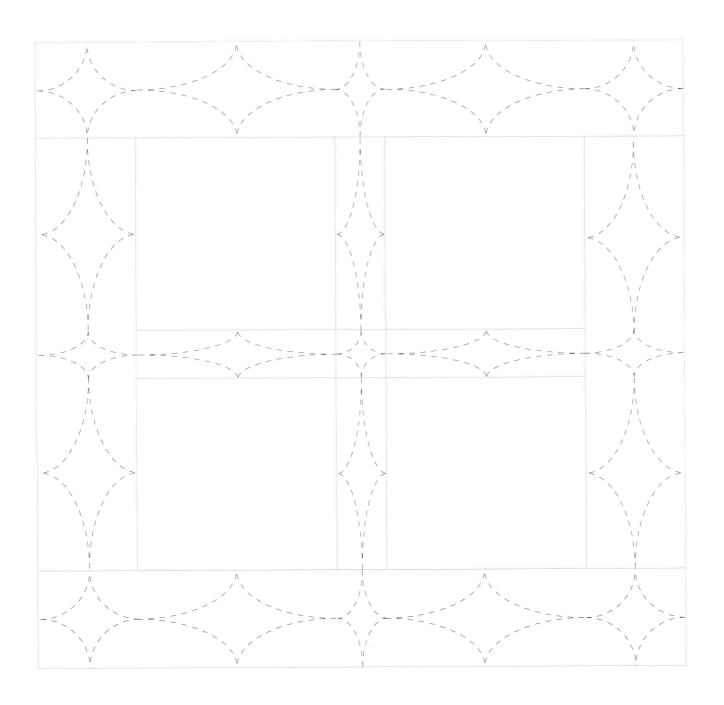

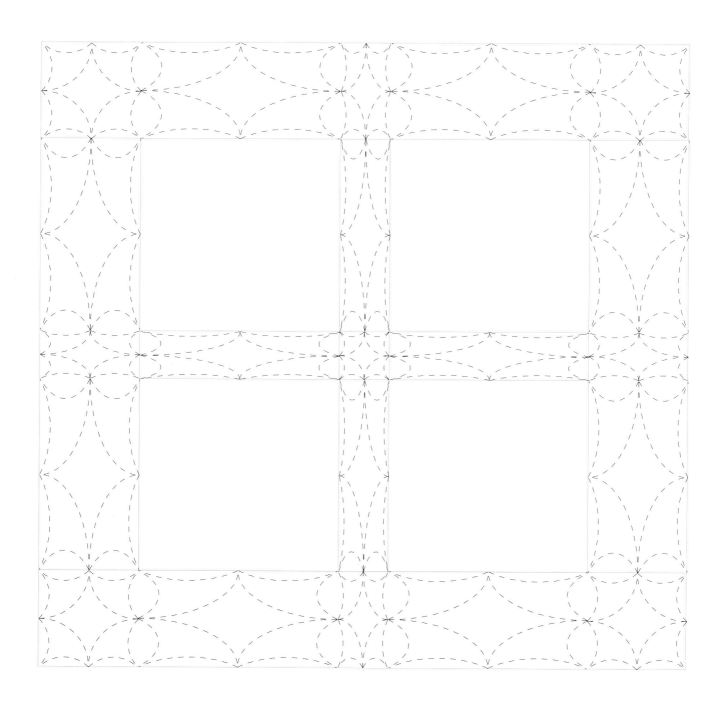

MARKING METHODS AND MARKERS

After deciding what to quilt comes the question of how to translate those decisions onto the fabric. Like everything else in quilting it is essentially a case of being aware of the options and building up confidence with practice. The only flaw in this sweeping statement is that we all want to get things right at the very first try and not have any disasters on our hands.

Most of us feel more comfortable with the concept of having the whole project marked up before putting the three quilt layers together and it is true that working with only one layer offers the greater number of options when it comes to choosing a marker and method of marking. On the other hand, it is neither impossible nor difficult to mark designs onto a project once it is basted and ready to go, and there may well be times when you are not ready to make design decisions before this point is reached.

If you are working with a single layer it is reasonably straightforward to smooth it out over a hard, flat (and preferably clean!) surface and tape or secure it in position so it doesn't shift while you are marking. Having all three layers together means that you either secure them as tautly and smoothly as possible on the aforementioned hard, flat surface, or you can mark section by section using a quilting hoop or frame to keep the layers at an even and high tension.

With only one layer to consider, the two main options are tracing through from a pattern placed underneath or marking directly onto the fabric either freehand or using templates or stencils. Where three layers are involved, their density means that the tracing-through option is not available, restricting you to marking directly onto the fabric by whatever means.

Tracing

Tracing is a skill most of us are encouraged to develop at an early age and, as a marking method, has a high comfort rating for most quilters – just follow the lines!

For best results with this method, you will need to have your pattern drawn out on white or translucent paper with a medium-point black pen. Secure the pattern sheet on a smooth hard surface at a comfortable working height, position the quilt top over it, and use masking tape to keep the quilt top from shifting as you mark. If your fabrics are predominantly pale, you should be able to see the majority of the pattern lines well enough to be able to trace them through with your chosen marker. For predominantly dark fabrics you will need to use a light box, or some similar arrangement of light source and transparent surface, underneath your pattern to enable you to see the lines for tracing. Either way, do your best to trace in a consistent and systematic sequence – nothing is more irritating and frustrating than lifting the fabric away from the pattern and finding that you have not traced all the lines, because it is nearly always impossible to replace the fabric and realign it perfectly. Tracing systematically is especially important if you are working with a light box – the light shining towards you means you are unable to see which lines you have already marked. Also you may find that you use a heavier pressure when marking over a light box or its equivalent simply because it is difficult to see and assess the strength of the lines you are making on the fabric.

Stencils and templates

Stencils are a very popular tool for marking onto fabric. What could be simpler than positioning the stencil and marking along all the channels, then lift, reposition the stencil as necessary and continue to mark until the pattern is complete and the space filled? Just remember to complete and connect all the lines before you begin to quilt! There is a huge selection of quilting stencils for you to choose from, or you can make your own using a craft knife or a double-bladed knife and card or plastic. The advantage of stencils over templates is that all the lines are included and only need a little extra connecting afterwards, whereas templates define the outer pattern lines only and anything else has to be added freehand later. Somehow, the word "freehand" instils deep fear and distrust in many quilters, who feel that they will be unable to make the right sort of pattern lines in this way. Again, confidence comes with the proverbial practice, which can be done on scrap paper or fabric before getting to grips with a major project. If you want to repeat a simple shape several times, adhesive templates cut from clear library film and positioned on your "quilting in progress" will give you a well-defined edge to stitch around and can be re-used several times with the advantage of no markings to remove later. Freezer paper, so beloved of quilters for so many uses, will also make good temporary templates that can be ironed in position and marked around before removing.

Needletracking

This is an old-fashioned and well-proven marking method that is ideal for freehand marking or use with stencils or templates. When properly done it leaves a clear scored line on fabric and retains its visibility even with moderate handling, which makes it suitable for small projects or for large projects that will be worked on a traditional frame. And, of course, because there is no pigment involved, there is the distinct advantage of not needing removal afterwards.

For this method you can use either a large blunt-tipped needle or the updated version of the traditional Japanese hera. You will need to work on a thickly padded surface to allow a good depth of impression on the fabric. The hera in particular is excellent if you want to mark clear straight lines such as those for grids or crosshatching.

Markers

There is one golden rule when deciding which marker is most suitable for a particular project: Test Before You Use. You can read or listen to any amount of information about markers, but what matters is that it will work for you in the way that you want it to and, most importantly, be removable in the way you want. Just because your friend or your teacher recommends a particular type or brand does not necessarily mean that you will like it or that it will suit the way you work. It really is worth taking a little extra time to think things through and make that all-important test before going ahead and marking up an entire project, whether you are making a small wallhanging or a full-size quilt.

What is required of a marker is that it will make a fine crisp line that is visible at working distance and will be easy to remove when quilting is finished. A fine line is particularly important if you are working on a small-scale/miniature piece or a wallhanging so that your stitches do not wander across the thickness of the line – there is also less marking to remove at the end. Absence of markings from a finished piece of quilting is a relatively new requirement – way back when quilts were commonplace household textiles, it was expected that markings would eventually disappear after two or three launderings. Nowadays our expectations and demands are somewhat different, being strongly influenced by the judging rules for competitive quilt shows.

The ideal marker would be easy to use, produce a fine line that stayed visible until the last stitch, and then magically render itself invisible without further effort. Sadly, no such thing exists. However, there is a wide selection of markers, each with its own characteristics, for you to choose from. Some of them are described below.

Pencil

Regular pencil is probably the most easily available marker and is visible on most pale fabrics. Opinions vary as to which is better – a hard lead or a soft. A hard lead pencil such as H or 2H will sharpen to an excellent point, hold this point well, and make a fine line that is barely visible after quilting. A light hand is required in terms of pressure; otherwise, you may inadvertently pull or drag the fabric slightly as you mark. A softer lead pencil will glide more easily over the fabric but loses its sharpness quickly and also leaves more graphite on the fabric to be removed later. Mechanical or propelling pencils can be a good choice, if only because they make a fine line without the need for sharpening - again a light hand is required to avoid the dreaded drag factor. There is an excellent mechanical pencil developed especially for quilters that is now available in a choice of colours – ask at your quilt shop for the Ultimate Marking pencil.

Chalk

If you are working with predominantly dark fabrics and want markings that will brush away, then chalk might be your first choice. Tailor's chalk may make too broad a line, but chalk wheels dispense powdered chalk with a delicious noise and a fine line that has enough staying power to allow you to mark a little and stitch a little. Refills are available in red, yellow and blue to allow you to use these gadgets on a wide range of fabric values. You could also try a soapstone pencil, which is easy to handle and can be sharpened to make a fine temporary line.

Water-soluble pen

Once hailed as the answer to every quilter's prayers for the ideal marker, this blue marker is visible on a wide range of fabric values and is removed afterwards by complete immersion in cold water. It is now available in two thicknesses, regular and fine. Take care not to expose your marked work to any form of heat, because it is possible that the marks will "set" permanently and be impossible to remove.

Fadeout pen

This magenta-coloured marker is chemically formulated to fade out and disappear from view over a short period of time, sometimes just a few hours. Fading occurs more rapidly in a dry atmosphere, and you may find that the unpredictability of the fading time makes this marker suitable only if you are prepared to mark a little, stitch a little. Take care to clean your work thoroughly after completion – the chemicals may not be visible but should be removed to avoid any future damage to the fabrics.

Quilter's pencils

These are available in several brands and colours, notably white and yellow. Test carefully on your chosen fabrics beforehand – some of these pencils have a high wax content that can make the marks difficult to remove.

Dressmaker's carbon

New formulations have improved the removeability of this established transfer film, which is suitable for use with templates, freehand marking or tracing over a drawn-out pattern. As with other markers, pre-testing for removal is strongly advised.

Water-soluble crayons and pens

Anything that is labelled as water soluble probably is just that – soluble in water with the emphasis on "in" rather than "with". Pre-test all water soluble crayons and pens on the fabrics you plan to use to check that the marks will come out when immersed for a short time in cold or cool water. If used sufficiently lightly, it may be possible to remove marks by sponging rather than soaking, but again you need to test it beforehand. Remember that these crayons and pens were developed for use primarily on paper, not fabric, which is more absorbent and so may take up more of the pigment.

Masking tape

A great way of "marking" straight lines without leaving any imprint on the fabric! Position lengths of masking tape so that you can quilt along one or both edges and then lift off the tape. If you avoid the temptation to leave the tape in position for more than a few hours, you will also avoid the problem of how to remove sticky residue from your fabric later on.

Other useful marking tools

Compasses, flexicurves and rulers will all make useful additions to your marking armoury – with these you can draft circular patterns, curves and straight lines directly onto the fabric either before or after basting.

Whichever marking method and/or marker you finally choose, remember that in the latter stages of a large project that has been much handled, it will be virtually impossible to see the original markings and lines. Try to approach this in a spirit of "refreshing" the marks rather than remaking them – it sounds so much more positive and encouraging!

HAND AND MACHINE QUILTING

At some point during the "how do I quilt it" questioning, you may find yourself pondering the "hand or machine" dilemma – which of the two techniques will be more appropriate to your project, which is easier, and so on. Your solutions will be based on your own preferences and experience, and also the type of patterns you plan to quilt.

Hand quilting has a softer, more traditional appearance, while machine quilting offers well-defined stitching and texture. One is not superior to the other – they are different techniques, and both need time and practice for good results. Machine quilting is not necessarily quicker than its handworked counterpart; speed for both techniques depends on the amount of quilting, type of patterns, and familiarity with the process. Basic outline quilting, straight line and continuous line patterns are all ideal candidates for machine quilting if you have only a moderate amount of experience. Hand quilting perhaps offers more scope for less experience, although I would have to declare an interest here as a hand quilter first and machine quilter second. Nonetheless it is surprising how much effective machine quilting can be achieved with only a small amount of experience and the use of a walking foot that allows all three layers to be fed evenly under the needle. You could of course use both techniques in the same piece – outlining by machine and filling in by hand – and get the best of both worlds.

Thread

Whichever means of quilting you choose, it is worth giving some consideration to your choice of thread. Using a thread fractionally darker in tone than the fabric is one way you can enhance the texture of the finished piece. This is easy to do if there are large expanses of fabric, but not so straightforward if you will be quilting over a gazillion tiny multi-coloured pieces. For the latter scenario it might be better to choose a neutral coloured thread (such as pale grey or a dark cream) for hand quilting or a fine "invisible" monofilament thread for machine quilting.

Choosing between brands and types of thread is pretty much a case of experimenting to see what suits you best from the huge selection that is available. It is worth noting that, with one or two exceptions, the majority of quilting threads are too thick for successful machine use, and most metallic threads need a degree of care whether you are quilting by hand or machine.

Needles

The rise and rise in popularity of the sewing machine for piecing appliqué and quilting has led to an awareness of the need to change needles more than twice in a lifetime – frequent changing of the machine needle means better results and fewer interesting clunking noises as you stitch. Machine needles are cheap and easily available in great variety. The same applies to hand quilting needles. They are the cheapest and most essential of tools, and yet the quilter's traditional thriftiness seems to prevent us from picking up a new needle for each new project, as we are advised to do with our sewing machines. When I suggest to a class that they could pick up a fresh needle each time they sit down to hand quilt, there is usually a stunned silence! It seems so wasteful, and yet if you work out the cost per use, it is minimal and you will have the advantage of always stitching with a sharp smooth needle that glides through the layers, rather than one which is perhaps bent and lacking in both sharpness of point and a full coating.

Hoops, frames and gizmos

Is it necessary to use a hoop or frame for hand quilting? Yes and no – most people find that, with the requisite amount of perseverance (otherwise called practice), the overall appearance of their work is improved by using a hoop or frame. Equally, it is possible to achieve show-winning quilting without either, but here the secret lies in the preparation, ie stretching and basting, of the layers before quilting. A hoop or frame will maintain the tension of the layers as you stitch. Quilting without one means that you must maintain this tension as you stitch.

For machine quilting there is now a wonderful gizmo in the form of a half-hoop with handles that sits on top of the work and helps you to guide and move it around under the needle. There is also a popular domestic version of the large industrial quilting frames.

B and B, or batting and basting

Batting

One of the delights of the wonderful world of quilting is that each year the variety of batting increases. Whereas it used to be simply a choice between 2oz or 4oz polyester batting, we now have a dazzling and sometimes confusing array of types and weights of battings to choose from – cotton, cotton/polyester mixes, all polyester, wool, silk, with scrim and without, needlepunched – the list just goes on. Rather than launch into a torrent of detail on battings, here are some general pointers for your consideration.

Buy the best you can afford. Branded goods are likely to be of a better quality than anonymous and unbranded batting from a roll at the back of a shop.

Thicker is not necessarily better – you will get a reasonable degree of loft (depth of texture) from even the thinnest of battings, and thick batting can be difficult to handle and work with.

Needlepunched battings are great for machine quilting but may not be so easy to stitch through when hand quilting.

All battings benefit from being spread out flat for a day or so before you use them, particularly if they have been pre-cut and packaged.

Cotton battings have a little more needle resistance than polyester, wool or silk battings.

Cotton and polyester battings are more laundry-friendly than wool.

An all-cotton batting is most suitable for fairly close quilting, either by hand or machine, and will give an average "loft" and a traditional feel to the finished piece.

Some cotton battings may need additional preparation before use so be sure to check the instructions before using.

Basting

Basting is still the chore all quilters love to hate, and most of us would do housework in preference to the tedium of basting. However you quilt, you must baste the three layers together by some means so that they will not shift while you are quilting. The only exception is if you hand quilt on a large traditional frame where the layers are attached to the bars of the frame and rolled taut.

So here are some general points on basting:

All three layers should be as smooth and taut as possible before you begin. This usually involves spreading out over the floor or a table top.

You can baste in a grid, sunburst or even a spiral formation – whichever you choose try to keep a distance of no more than three inches between the basting lines.

It is usual to baste from the centre of the piece and work towards the outer edges so any movement of the layers is outwards.

For hand quilting you can baste with long straight stitches, small safety pins or use a basting gun that shoots plastic tags through the layers. All three methods work well if you observe the "more is better" rule and keep the layers smooth.

For sheer speed and ease of getting a boring job done, the basting gun is hard to beat, but the little tags seem to multiply while holding the layers together so there are even more of them to remove after quilting!

For machine quilting you may prefer to choose between small safety pins, the basting gun or a spray adhesive to hold the layers together – basting stitches have an annoying habit of getting caught up in the toe of the machine foot, or of being difficult to remove completely afterwards. If the spray adhesive option appeals, be sure to use one that is suitable for use on fabric – ask at your local quilt shop rather than the nearest hardware store.

Selected bibliography

The Essential Quilter   Barbara Chainey   David & Charles 1993

The Essential Quilter Project Book   Barbara Chainey   David & Charles 1997

Quilting with Style   Gwen Marston & Joe Cunningham   American Quilter's Society 1993

Quilting Makes the Quilt   Lee Cleland   That Patchwork Place 1994

Machine Quilting Made Easy   Maurine Noble   That Patchwork Place 1994

Acknowledgements

Personal

Derek and Anna, who have both remained calm and unruffled throughout numerous panics, tantrums, absence and lack of attention to basic domestic details; Pat and Mike, who have given me more encouragement than I deserve; Maggie and Alan, Chris, Cath, Pat, JeanAnn, Elaine and Di, Lynne, Margaret and George, Sandie and Dave, Ann Roberts, Pam Lewis, Heather and Ann, Asher and Priscilla – my grateful thanks to all of you.

Editorial

Cheryl Brown again proved the very model of a supportive editor; Brenda Morrison, unflappable to the last; Maggi McCormick, who not only worked her by now traditional copy editing magic but gave invaluable advice and encouragement during the early stages, Glynis Edwards who made it possible to put a jumble of illustrations and text into a coherent layout.

Illustrations

An enormous bouquet of thanks to Diane Redgate, who never wavered or flinched even in the face of lengthy faxes and imprecise instructions, and without whose patience and computer skills this book would most certainly not exist; Penny McMorris for her support and permissions connected with the wonderful Electric Quilt program; Lawrence Dawes, whose infectious enthusiasm for computer quilt programs first encouraged me to explore their possibilities.

Quilts

Sally Radway, Jacquie Taylor, Mandy Fanthom, Patricia Cox, Ann King, Shirley Prescott, Sandie Lush, Susie Corke, Jenny Otto, Rosalind Leslie, Elaine Hammond, Martha Preston, Vivienne Coles, Mary Christie, Joan Loudon and Maggie Alexander for making quilts, quilting tops, finishing quilts, and also loaning quilts.

All at Rose & Hubble, particularly Maggie and Sharon.

All the staff and students at The Bramble Patch in Northampton and Purely Patchwork in Linlithgow who responded so magnificently to my garbled request for help and efficiently put together a satisfyingly large pool of quilts to select from. And, of course, all students and quilters who have ever asked the question "How do I quilt it?"

INDEX

Entries in *italic* indicate photographs

Amish-style quilts, 9, 142-145,
    appliqué, blocks, 26-29,
    quilts, 58-59, 70-71, 81-88,
    107-116, 166-172 ·
Attic Windows, block, 20,
    quilt, 53, 55

background quilting, 22, 26, 64,
    72, 104, 146
Baptist Fan, 118
Basket quilt, 37, 56, 101-103
basting, 189
batting, 189
blocks, appliqué, 26-29,
    combinations of, 64-89,
    117, 118-123, curved seam,
    22-25, definition of, 12,
    foundation-pieced, 31,
    individual, 12-31, log cabin,
    30-31, pieced, 14-21, plain,
    72-89, 102-103, 104-116,
    quilting patterns, for, 176-
    182, settings, edge to edge,
    42- 63 medallion, 104-117,
    on point, 90-103 sampler,
    118-123, strip-pieced, 30-31
borders, 104-116, 120-123, 146-
    172, 182-183
braided quilts, 132-135

cable, 9, 105, 142
clamshell, 9, 118, 142, 146
corded quilting, 105
crosshatch quilting, 104, 118,
    142, 146

Double Wedding Ring, block, 25,
    quilt, 60-61
Dresden Plate, block, 4,
    quilt, 154-159
Drunkard's Path, block, 23,
    quilt, 62, 160-161

echo quilting, 22, 26, *33, 118*

feather swags, 105, 110
feather wreath, 83-84, *90,* 102,
    145
feathered cable, 9, 144
fiddlehead fern, 145
foundation-pieced blocks, 31, 36,
    43, 124

four point star, block, 15
    quilt, 41, 51, 66-69, 80,
    94-100, 117
freezer paper, 186

Grandmother's fan, block, 2,
grid, *see* crosshatch

halving principle, 9, 10, 64, *72,*
    146
hexagons, 139-141

Inner City, 137-138, *139*

kaleidoscope, block, 18,
    quilt, 150-151

light box, 185
Log Cabin block, 30 quilt, *125,*
    126-128, 162-165

machine quilting, *85*
Mariner's Compass, block, 31,
    quilt, 36, 63, 149
marking, patterns, 185-186
marking tools, 186-187
meander quilting, 8, 26, *65,*
    110-111
medallion quilts, appliqué, 107-
    116, pieced, 104-106
motifs, quilting patterns, 176,
    scale, 10, 72

needles, 188
needletracking, 186

Oak Leaf and Reel, block, 29,
    quilt, 107-112, 169-172,
    quilting pattern, 76, 79, 89
Ohio Star, block, 15, quilt, 47, 76,
    92-93, 106, 117
Orange Peel, block, 22 quilt, 89
outline quilting, 10, 14, 26, *118*

Palm Leaf, quilt, 40
Pansy, block, 21, quilt, 151
paper cutting, 10, 72, *73*
patterns, quilting, 176-185
pumpkin seed, 144

quilt frames, 188
quilt hoops, 188
quilting, direction, 8, 148,
    lines, curved, 11, 14, 22,
    straight, 11, 14, 22, *90,*
    patterns, 176-184,

quilting, direction (continued)
        see also baptist fan, cable,
        clamshell, feather,
        feathered cable, feathered
        wreath, pumpkin seed,
        spider web, wineglass,

Rail Fence, block, 30,
    quilt, 128, *129,* 130, 153
reducing glass, 32
rippling, 148
Roman Stripe, block, 31,
    quilt, 128, 129, 131, 152,
    ruler, 148, 187

safety pins, 189
sampler quilts, 118-123
sashing, 101, 121-123, 148,
    173-175, 183-184
Schoolhouse, block, 21
seam lines, 30, 31, 124, 128, 137,
    see also outline quilting
spacer blocks, *see* blocks, plain
spider web, 10, 113
Spinning Star, block, 16,
    quilt, *42,* 44-46
spray adhesive, 189
square within a square, block,
    19, quilt, 39, 48-50
stencils, 185
stitching direction, 8, 148
Storm at Sea, block, 20, quilt, 57
strip-pieced blocks, 30,
    quilts, 128-135
Sunbonnet Sue, block, 26,
    quilt, 70, 81, 166-167

tacking, *see* basting
templates, 185
thread, 188
Tumbling Blocks, 136
Turkey Tracks, block, 27,
    quilt, 58-59, 71, 174-175
tying, 137

vermicelli quilting, *see* meander
    quilting
visualising quilting patterns, 10

wadding, *see* batting
Wineglass, 9, 142, 146